GIGGLING SQUID

Tantalising Thai to cook at home

GIGGLING SQUID

SQUID

Tantalising Thai to cook at home

EBURY
PRESS

CONTENTS

INTRODUCTION

Food has always played a central role in my life. My earliest and often favourite childhood memories of growing up in Thailand always seem to focus on food. Thailand is teeming with natural resources – beautiful herbs, spices and vegetables – and being quite an adventurous kid, I spent many happy hours climbing trees to pick mangoes and tamarind and occasionally helping myself to a handful of glossy red chillies growing on my neighbours' land on the banks of the Mekong River!

The inspiration behind our Giggling Squid menus and the recipes included here comes from traditional Thai dishes but also a lifelong fascination with natural ingredients – instilled in me from childhood trips with my mum to our local food markets. I'd wander past tubs of live prawns, glistening rows of fresh fish packed in ice, bundles of green leafy vegetables, baskets of colourful fruits and small, sizzling grills with all manner of delicious treats – my favourite being Moo Ping pork skewers.

It's not simply the rich variety of ingredients that defines Thai food – it's also how we eat our meals. In Thailand, we don't really have the concept of starters and mains, it's all about serving an array of different dishes to bring balance to the meal, and we'll often choose a soup, stir-fry and spicy salad to offer that variety. Most importantly, it's about sharing and enjoying the dishes together and, in that sense, even a simple family dinner becomes an occasion. It was a longing to bring this spirit of Thai mealtimes to the UK that inspired me and my husband Andy to create Giggling Squid.

I moved to the UK to study in Brighton and in my spare time I waitressed at a local Thai restaurant, which is when I fell in love with the restaurant business (Andy, too, but that's a different story), with its buzz, fast pace and that sense of fulfilment when your guests are relishing their food. Mealtimes in Thailand are sociable and super relaxed – there's no standing on ceremony! It's all about good food and good company and this is what I wanted to bring to the UK food scene.

Andy and I opened our first Thai restaurant in Brighton in a tiny, rickety fisherman's cottage with dodgy electricity and the kitchen in the basement, with Andy and I taking turns to wash up. Our first ever Thai tapas menu is still going strong in our restaurants today and I have now been in the hospitality business for over 20 years, which I can't quite believe. And of course, the question we are always asked… the name Giggling Squid was originally the nickname for one of our three kids (we're not allowed to say which one!).

I hope you enjoy trying out the recipes. People sometimes express a nervousness when approaching Thai cooking because they are unfamiliar with some of the ingredients. I always give the same advice: 'Hot and fast and don't forget to have fun!'. If you can't find the exact ingredient, experiment and don't be afraid to add your own personal touch. Enjoy.

Pranee

Co-founder

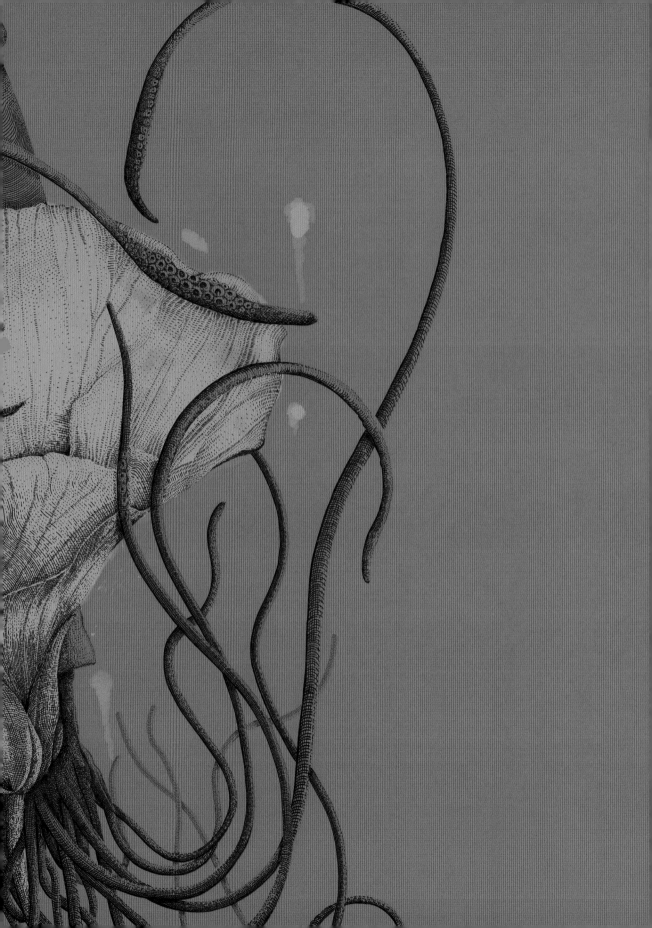

THAI
TAPAS

Forget food envy, Thai tapas is the perfect way to indulge in the variety of textures and flavours that Thailand's food is known for. This way everyone gets a little taste of everything.

These found their way onto our menu by popular demand as we used to only offer them as canapés at opening parties for new restaurants. But people loved the crisp pastry and the herby chicken filling, and they're now one of our most most-requested dishes.

GOLDEN MONEY BAGS

Makes 16, to serve 4

250g minced chicken
1 carrot, peeled and cut into small dice
1 spring onion, finely sliced
1 medium potato, peeled and cut into small dice
4 tbsp freshly chopped coriander
2 tsp salt
4 tsp cracked black pepper
4 tsp granulated sugar
4 tbsp Stir-fry Sauce (see recipe below)
500ml vegetable or rapeseed oil, plus
   extra for greasing
5 sheets of spring roll pastry
200ml sweet chilli sauce, to serve

For the Stir-fry Sauce (Makes a batch of 900ml)
400ml water
250g granulated sugar
500ml light soy sauce
30g cornflour or potato starch

To make the Stir-fry Sauce, mix all the ingredients together in a pan over a low heat until the sugar and cornflour have dissolved. Leave to cool and store in the fridge for up to two weeks.

Put the chicken in a large mixing bowl, add the vegetables, coriander, salt, pepper, sugar and stir-fry sauce and mix well.

Lightly grease your hands with oil and form the mixture into 16 equal, round meatballs, reserving a little to test the oil. Cut 4 sheets of spring roll pastry into 4 equal pieces to create 16 rectangles. Place a meatball in the centre of each piece of pastry and wrap into a pouch. Cut the remaining sheet of spring roll pastry into long strings and use one to tie the money bag together at the top. Repeat with the remaining meatballs and spring roll pastry – you should have 16 money bags in total.

Pour the oil into a wok or deep saucepan and heat over a medium to high heat. To test if the oil is hot enough, add a small meatball. If the oil sizzles and the meatball starts to colour quickly, it is ready.

Place the money bags into the hot oil and deep-fry for 4–5 minutes until golden brown. You may need to do this in batches, depending on the size of your pan.

Serve 4 money bags per person with 50ml of the sweet chilli sauce on the side for dipping.

There's just something about the sight and aroma of chicken satay skewers lined up on a small open grill in a street market. Often, it's the first scent that greets you in the taxi ride from the airport as you touch down in Thailand.

CHICKEN SATAY

Makes 16, to serve 4

320g chicken breast, cut into 20g slices
2 tbsp crushed garlic
4 tsp ground turmeric
2 tsp curry powder
4 tsp salt
2 tsp cracked black pepper
2 tbsp granulated sugar
2 tbsp freshly chopped coriander
4 tbsp honey
4 tbsp evaporated milk
16 short bamboo skewers

To serve
175ml sweet chilli sauce
4 tbsp roasted unsalted peanuts, crushed

Put the chicken in a large mixing bowl and add the remaining ingredients. Mix well and leave to marinate in the fridge for 2 hours.

Soak the bamboo skewers in cold water for 10 minutes.

Thread each piece of marinated chicken on to a prepared skewer.

Heat a griddle pan over a medium to high heat, add the skewers and grill for 1 minute each side – 4 minutes in total. You may need to do this in batches, depending on the size of your pan.

Mix the sweet chilli sauce with the crushed peanuts and serve alongside the chicken satay skewers.

Jicama is gently sweet with a fresh crunch, so it teams up perfectly with the burst of flavours in this salad. It's worth the effort to track down but apples make a good substitute too.

SWEET JICAMA OR APPLE SALAD VG

Serves 4

300g tamarind juice

100g granulated sugar

4 tsp salt

4 tbsp light soy sauce

4 pinches of chilli flakes

250g sliced jicama or apple

½ red onion, sliced

2 carrots, peeled and cut into matchsticks

2 spring onions, finely sliced

4 tbsp freshly chopped coriander

2 tbsp freshly sliced mint leaves

4 tsp Fried Onions, to serve
   (see Ingredients, page 198)

Add the tamarind, sugar, salt, soy sauce and chilli flakes to a large mixing bowl and mix together to make a sauce.

In a separate bowl, add the jicama (or apple), red onion, carrots, spring onions, coriander and mint and fold them in until all the ingredients are well mixed.

Now add the sauce and gently mix together, ensuring all the vegetables are coated with it. Transfer to a serving platter or large plate. Top with the fried onion to serve.

For many people a spring roll with its flaky pastry and hot, tasty filling is the ultimate everyday comfort food. They are also frequently made to share with friends and family on special occasions.

SPRING ROLLS VG

Makes 12, to serve 4

500ml vegetable or rapeseed oil, for deep-frying, plus 8 tbsp
½ sweetheart cabbage, finely shredded
200g carrots, thinly sliced into matchsticks
2 celery sticks, thinly sliced into matchsticks
1 large leek, thinly sliced into matchsticks
4 tsp salt
½ tsp ground white pepper
4 tsp granulated sugar
8 tbsp Stir-fry Sauce (see page 12)
4 tbsp freshly chopped coriander
12 sheets of filo pastry
Sweet chilli sauce, to serve

Batter mix to seal the pastry
50g self-raising flour or plain flour
20ml water

Add the 8 tablespoons of oil to a wok and place over a medium to high heat. Add all the vegetables, followed by the salt, pepper, sugar, stir-fry sauce and coriander and stir-fry for 2 minutes. Remove from the heat and set aside to cool. Once cool, chill in the fridge for 1 hour.

To make the spring rolls, use one sheet of pastry for each spring roll to ensure maximum crispiness.

Place about 45g of the vegetable filling in the centre of each piece of pastry. Carefully roll the pastry over the top of the filling, tucking in both ends halfway through rolling.

Combine the flour and water to make a batter mix, then use this to carefully seal the ends of the rolls.

Pour the 500ml oil into a wok or deep saucepan over a medium to high heat. Add the spring rolls and deep-fry for 4–5 minutes or until golden brown. You may need to do this in batches, depending on the size of your pan.

Remove the cooked spring rolls to paper towels to soak up any excess oil, then serve with sweet chilli sauce for dipping.

Another delicious and popular street-food treat from Bangkok. Pork belly can sometimes be a bit under-valued but this combination with the black pepper works so well to bring out the sweetness of the meat.

BLACK PEPPER PORK BELLY

Serves 4

800g pork belly, diced
300ml Stir-fry Sauce (see page 12)
150g granulated sugar
1 tsp cracked black pepper
8 tbsp light soy sauce
4 tbsp crushed garlic
500ml vegetable or rapeseed oil
12 little gem lettuce leaves

Put the pork belly in a large mixing bowl and add the stir-fry sauce, sugar, black pepper, soy sauce and crushed garlic. Mix well and leave to marinate in the fridge for 2 hours.

Heat the oil in a wok over a medium to high heat, add the marinated pork belly and deep – fry for 4 minutes until golden brown. Remove to a plate and set aside.

Carefully decant the oil into a heatproof container, reserving a teaspoon for the next cooking stage. Return the wok to the heat and add the leftover marinade. Cook until the sauce thickens – about 1 minute – then return the pork belly to the pan and toss through to coat.

Divide the pork belly equally among the lettuce leaves and serve immediately.

Nothing beats the perfect balance of flavours in a traditional papaya salad – savoury, fresh and with a satisfying flash of spicy heat.

SOM TAM – GREEN PAPAYA SALAD VG

Serves 4

4 tbsp light soy sauce

8 tbsp granulated sugar

2 tsp salt

8 tbsp tamarind juice

2 tsp crushed garlic

1 lime, halved

2 bird's eye chillies, whole with stalks removed

200g green papaya, thinly sliced into matchsticks

120g carrots, thinly sliced into matchsticks

20 fine green beans, halved

4 cherry tomatoes, halved

8 little gem lettuce leaves

Put the soy sauce, sugar, salt and tamarind in a large mixing bowl and mix well.

Using a pestle and mortar, pound the crushed garlic, lime and chillies together. Remove the lime skin before adding the rest of the ingredients.

Add the papaya, carrots and fine beans to a mixing bowl and mix them together using a large spoon. Then mix in the pounded garlic, lime and chilli.

Pour in the tamarind mixture and fold in, then stir through the cherry tomatoes.

Divide in the salad equally between the lettuce leaves to serve.

There's something so immediately satisfying and a little theatrical about eating with your hands and these little nests are best enjoyed without cutlery. Simply wrap the lettuce leaves around the goodies and devour in one mouthful!

VEGGIE GOODIE BOWLS VG

Serves 4

300ml tamarind juice
100g palm sugar (or soft brown sugar)
2 tsp salt
4 tsp light soy sauce
60g diced pineapple
75g whole chestnuts, diced
75g water chestnuts, diced
1 green apple, diced
6 tbsp Fried Onions
   (see Ingredients, page 198)
16 little gem lettuce leaves

Put the tamarind juice, sugar, salt and soy sauce in a large mixing bowl and mix well. Add the pineapple, chestnuts, water chestnuts, apple and fried onions to the dressing and toss together.

Arrange the lettuce leaves on a large platter or individual serving plates and divide the salad equally between them.

A decadent pork belly dish, sweet, sticky and caramelised. You can also wrap this hot candy pork in a sticky ball of rice (see page 143) before eating.

CANDY PORK WITH PINEAPPLE

Serves 4

500ml vegetable or rapeseed oil

800g pork belly, diced

300ml Stir-fry Sauce (see page 12)

100g granulated sugar

4 tbsp sriracha sauce

1 tbsp light soy sauce

300ml tamarind juice

300g diced pineapple

1 red pepper deseeded and sliced

4 tbsp Fried Onions
   (see Ingredients, page 198)

Heat the oil in a wok over a medium to high heat, add the pork belly and deep-fry for 4 minutes until golden brown. Remove the pork to a plate and set aside.

Carefully decant the oil into a heatproof container, reserving a tablespoon for the next cooking stage. Return the oil to a medium to high heat and add the Stir-fry Sauce, sugar, sriracha, soy sauce and tamarind juice and cook until glossy, then add the pineapple, red pepper and pork belly and stir-fry for a further minute.

Transfer to a serving plate or divide between four plates, garnish with the fried onions and serve.

This is a recipe to make your mouth water. We use a typical 'seafood sauce' made from fish sauce, chilli, garlic, spring onions and lemongrass to flavour the prawns, and it's an absolute favourite.

ZINGY PRAWNS

Serves 4

50g butter salted or unsalted (depending
    on preference)
12 tbsp crushed garlic
200g large, uncooked prawns

For the dressing
12 tbsp fish sauce
8 tbsp granulated sugar
12 tbsp lime juice
4 tbsp crushed red chillies
12 tbsp crushed garlic
4 tbsp freshly chopped coriander
1 spring onion, finely sliced
1 lemongrass stick, finely sliced

First make the garlic butter. Mash together the butter and minced garlic and set aside.

Add 1 tablespoon of the garlic butter to a flat or griddle pan on medium to high heat and fry the prawns until cooked through. Grill the prawns on a griddle pan for 2 minutes until cooked through.

Place the fish sauce, sugar, lime juice, chilli, garlic and coriander in a mixing bowl and mix well. Now add the spring onion and lemongrass, folding into the dressing.

Divide the cooked prawns between four plates and drizzle over some dressing to serve. Serve the remaining dressing in a bowl on the side so people can add more if they like.

One of the best culinary activities is visiting the local seafood markets in Thailand where produce is so fresh it barely needs any other ingredients. This recipe was inspired by that pleasing simplicity – the fresh sweetness of squid fried with aromatic garlic.

GARLICKY GRILLED SQUID

Serves 4

4 tsp ground turmeric

4 tsp mild curry powder

2 tsp salt

4 tbsp Stir-fry Sauce (see page 12)

4 tsp granulated sugar

4 tbsp crushed garlic

500g squid, cut into 20 pieces and scored

2 tbsp fried garlic

180ml sweet chilli sauce, to serve

For the fried garlic

100ml vegetable or rapeseed oil

3 garlic cloves, finely sliced

Put the turmeric, curry powder, salt, stir-fry sauce, sugar and crushed garlic in a large mixing bowl and mix well. Add the squid, mix well and leave to marinate in the fridge for 2 hours.

Remove the squid from the marinade and cook on a hot griddle pan for 3–4 minutes until evenly charred. You may need to do this in batches, depending on the size of your pan.

To make the fried garlic garnish, heat the vegetable or rapeseed oil to medium to high heat and fry the sliced garlic cloves to golden–brown colour. Remove from the heat and place on paper towels to remove excess oil.

Place the squid in a serving dish or on individual plates. Garnish with the fried garlic and serve with the chilli sauce alongside.

You'd never guess at the depth of flavour in these salmon nests. You'll love the look of delighted surprise on people's faces after they've put the whole morsel in their mouths and started to chew, discovering new flavours and textures with every bite.

SALMON MORSELS

Serves 4

4 tbsp self-raising flour

2 salmon fillets, skin on and diced into
    2.5cm (1-inch) cubes

500ml vegetable or rapeseed oil

4 tbsp sweet chilli sauce

4 tsp tamarind juice

4 tbsp sriracha sauce

16 little gem lettuce leaves

2 tsp diced fresh ginger

4 tbsp diced red onion

2 tbsp finely sliced lemongrass

4 tbsp diced lime

4 tbsp Fried Onions
    (see Ingredients, page 198)

Scatter the flour over a plate and dust the salmon cubes in it, making sure they are completely coated.

Heat the oil in a wok or deep saucepan over a medium to high heat, add the salmon and deep-fry for 1–1½ minutes. Remove and drain on paper towels.

Mix together the sweet chilli sauce, tamarind juice and sriracha sauce and set aside.

Arrange the lettuce leaves on a large platter or individual plates or ramekins and top with the salmon, followed by the ginger and red onion, lemongrass and lime. Drizzle a teaspoon of the sauce over each piece of salmon and garnish with fried onions.

We introduced these on a special menu to celebrate Veganuary and they proved so popular we couldn't part with them. They have such a pleasing flavour and texture with the satisfying crunch of sunflower seeds.

CORN FRITTERS VG

Makes 36, to serve 4

640g sweetcorn
4 tbsp self-raising flour
4 tbsp granulated sugar
4 tbsp freshly chopped coriander
8 tbsp cornflour
1 tsp salt
2 tsp cracked black pepper
150g sunflower seeds
500ml vegetable or rapeseed oil
180ml sweet chilli sauce, to serve

Blitz the sweetcorn to a rough paste in a food processor or blender. Transfer to a bowl, add the flour, sugar, coriander, cornflour and salt and pepper and mix until combined. Using your hands, shape the mixture into flat round discs approximately the size of a digestive biscuit and around 2cm in thickness.

Put the sunflower seeds into a bowl and dip each fritter into the seeds, pressing them on to the fritters so that they are completely coated.

Heat the oil in a wok or deep saucepan. To test if the oil is hot enough, add a small piece of fritter. If the oil sizzles and the fritter starts to colour quickly, it is ready. Add the fritters and deep-fry for 4 minutes until golden brown. You may need to do this in batches, depending on the size of your pan.

Serve with sweet chilli sauce alongside for dipping.

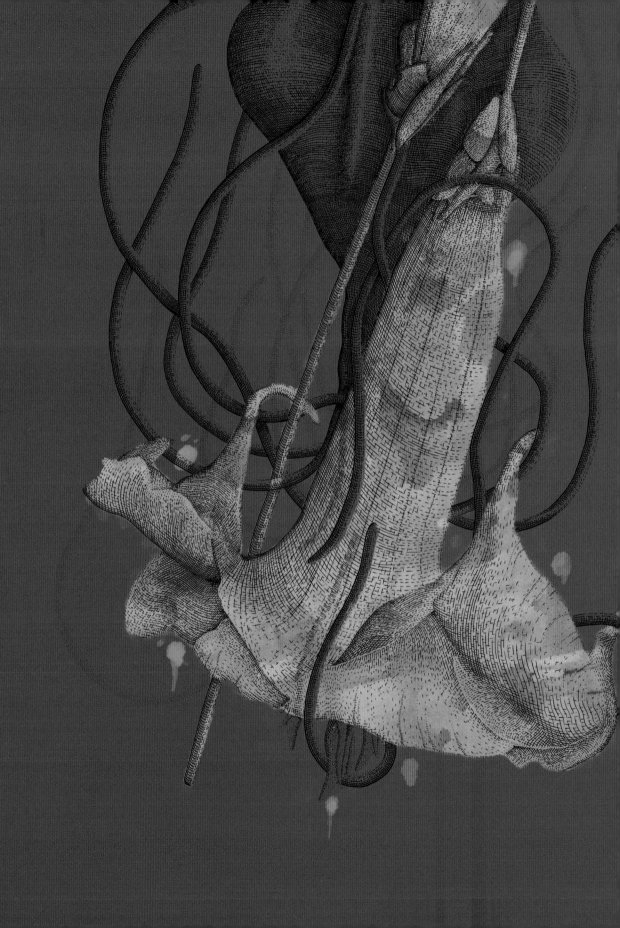

LIGHT
MEALS

We don't have specific breakfast dishes in Thailand
but tend to go for something light and delicately
flavoured like rice or noodle broths. The *Kuay Jab*
on page 44 is one of my favourites, so please do
give it a go – you won't be disappointed.

Thai rice soup is simple, delicious and comforting and often served as a medicinal pick-me-up when someone is feeling under the weather.

KHAO TOM WITH SPICY PRAWNS

Serves 2

500g cooked coconut rice (see page 140)

200ml water

1 chicken stock cube

Pinch of salt

3 tbsp vegetable or rapeseed oil

380g large, uncooked prawns

2 large garlic cloves, chopped

2 tbsp freshly chopped coriander

1 spring onion, sliced

1 tsp Fried Garlic
   (see Ingredients, page 198)

Pinch of chilli flakes, ground in a pestle and mortar

2 pinches of cracked black pepper

Place the cooked coconut rice and water into a saucepan over a high heat. Bring to the boil, add the chicken stock cube and salt and cook over a low heat for 2 minutes until thickened to a porridge-like consistency.

Add the oil to a flat non-stick pan over a medium to high heat, then add the prawns and chopped garlic and stir-fry until the prawns are pink.

Spoon the rice into two bowls, top with the prawns and garnish with the coriander, spring onion, fried garlic, chilli and pepper.

We can't get enough of this broth. It's rich and satisfying and the rolled rice noodles are so light and delicate – exactly the kind of dish to choose for breakfast or a light lunch from a local street stall.

KUAY JAB – ROLLED RICE NOODLES IN FIVE-SPICE BROTH

Serves 2

For the pork belly

200g pork belly strip

500ml water

1 tbsp Stir-fry Sauce (see page 12)

1 bay leaf

1 star anise

200ml vegetable or rapeseed oil

For the broth

400ml water

2 chicken stock cubes

2 tsp Chinese five spice

1 tsp cracked black pepper

4 tbsp Stir-fry Sauce (see page 12)

100g rice flakes, soaked in cold water for 2 hours and drained or 100g rice noodles

8 slices of cooked pork belly or 8 cooked prawns or both

1 pak choi, leaves separated

2 soft-boiled eggs, halved

1 spring onion, sliced

2 tbsp freshly chopped coriander

2 tsp Fried Onions (see Ingredients, page 198)

First cook the pork belly by heating the water in a saucepan on a medium to high heat, then add the stir-fry sauce, bay leaf and star anise and bring it to the boil. Add the pork belly strip and cook for 5 minutes.

Once cooked, remove the pork from the pan, and set aside to cool down for 5 minutes.

Next heat the oil in a flat round pan on medium heat and fry the pork belly strip until golden brown on all sides. Slice the pork belly strip in to 8 2-cm slices, and set aside.

For the broth add the water, chicken stock cubes, five spice, black pepper and stir-fry sauce to a wok. Bring to the boil over a medium to high heat and cook for 2 minutes.

Add the rice flakes or noodles and cook for 3 minutes until they are soft.

Add the sliced pork belly and/or cooked prawns and pak choi and cook for a further minute.

Divide into two bowls and garnish with soft-boiled egg, spring onion, coriander and Fried Onions.

A good Thai omelette is real comfort food – it isn't just for breakfast! It's a little different to its European counterpart and often eaten as a topper on a dish of rice or a side to take the edge off a spicy main dish.

THAI OMELETTE

Serves 2

4 eggs

4 tbsp cooked minced pork

6 tbsp sweetcorn

½ white onion, diced

1 pepper of any colour, deseeded and diced

4 tbsp Stir-fry Sauce (see page 12)

2 tbsp freshly chopped coriander

1 tsp ground white pepper

4 tbsp vegetable or rapeseed oil

Crack the eggs into a mixing bowl and whisk well. Add the pork, sweetcorn, onion, pepper, stir-fry sauce, coriander and white pepper and mix well.

Heat the oil in a flat non-stick frying pan over a medium to high heat, add the egg mixture and cook for 4–5 minutes on each side until light golden in colour.

We admit you won't find this in Thailand, but we've added a Thai twist to this classic British breakfast with edamame beans and a spicy kick.

THAI BEANS ON TOAST WITH AVOCADO vg

Serves 2

4 slices of bloomer bread
2 avocados, peeled and quartered
2 pinches of cracked black pepper

For the Thai beans
200g edamame beans
4 garlic cloves
2 tsp chopped red chilli
Drizzle of vegetable or rapeseed oil
6 tbsp ketchup
2 tsp freshly chopped Thai basil
1 tsp sliced lime leaves

Bring a saucepan of water to the boil over a medium to high heat, then add the edamame beans and cook for 4–5 minutes until the beans are tender. Drain and set aside.

Blend the garlic with red chilli in a small food processor or using a pestle and mortar.

Heat the oil in a flat non-stick frying pan over a medium to high heat and add the garlic chilli mix, ketchup, basil and lime leaves and cook for a minute, then add the cooked edamame beans and stir through.

Toast the bloomer bread on both sides in a toaster or under a hot grill. Divide between two plates and top the toast with the Thai beans and avocado quarters and garnish with the black pepper.

A dish all children seem to love – even the fussiest ones – so it's a bit of a lifesaver on a busy midweek evening when you're out of inspiration and the cupboard's a little bare.

DARK SOY PORK FRIED RICE

Serves 2

4 tbsp vegetable or rapeseed oil

2 tbsp crushed garlic

2 eggs, beaten

200g pork loin, sliced

½ white onion, diced

1 spring onion, sliced

1 pak choi, sliced and blanched

4 broccoli florets, halved and blanched

400g cooked coconut rice (see page 140)

1 tomato, sliced or diced

4 tbsp dark soy sauce

2 tbsp light soy sauce

2 tbsp granulated sugar

2 tbsp Stir-fry Sauce (see page 12)

Heat the oil in a wok over a medium to high heat, add the crushed garlic and beaten egg and stir-fry until cooked.

Add the pork and stir-fry along with the diced white onion, sliced spring onion, pak choi and broccoli until the pork is lightly brown and cooked.

Now add the cooked coconut rice, followed by the tomato, dark and light soy sauces, sugar and stir-fry sauce and toss it in the wok for 2 minutes until all the ingredients are thoroughly mixed.

Divide between two bowls and serve.

This is definitely not a Thai speciality, but I can't resist these gently sweet and fluffy pancakes with a drizzle of honey and the salty contrast of bacon.

COCONUT PANCAKES WITH BACON AND A POACHED EGG

Serves 2

6 slices of smoked streaky bacon
2 eggs
2 tbsp honey

For the coconut pancakes
250g self-raising flour
½ tsp baking powder
¼ tsp salt
1 egg
160ml milk, either whole or semi-skimmed
160ml coconut milk

To make the coconut pancakes, add the self-raising flour, baking powder and salt to a mixing bowl and mix well. Next, add the egg, milk and coconut milk and whisk until you have a smooth batter.

Heat an egg pan or a flat non-stick frying pan over a medium to high heat. Ladle about 50ml of the batter into the pan and cook the pancake for 1½ minutes each side. Repeat with the remaining mixture – you should have 8 pancakes in total.

Meanwhile, cook the bacon on a griddle pan until crisp.

To poach the eggs, bring a saucepan of water to a gentle simmer. Crack 1 egg into a small bowl and slip it into the boiling water. Turn off the heat, cover the pan with a lid and set a timer for 4 minutes. Remove the eggs with a slotted spoon and drain well.

Arrange 4 pancakes on each plate, top with 3 slices of crispy bacon and a poached egg and drizzle the honey over the top to serve.

This is my hubby Andy's favourite. He tried it on our first holiday to Thailand – one of the many local specialities I insisted he try! – and it remains one of his top three dishes.

TOM KHA – COCONUT CHICKEN SOUP

Serves 2

500ml water
50ml coconut milk
100g cooked chicken breast, sliced
4 tsp sliced lemongrass
4 slices of galangal
4 lime leaves, thinly sliced
½ red chilli, sliced
2 tsp chilli paste
6 oyster mushrooms, roughly torn
6 tbsp fish sauce
6 tbsp lime juice
2 tsp granulated sugar
2 cherry tomatoes, halved
4 tbsp freshly chopped coriander

Pour the water and coconut milk into a saucepan over a medium to high heat and bring to the boil.

Add the sliced chicken, lemongrass, galangal, lime leaves and chilli and cook for 3–4 minutes. Add the chilli paste, oyster mushrooms, fish sauce, lime juice and sugar and cook for a further 2 minutes.

Divide between two bowls, garnish with the cherry tomatoes and chopped coriander and serve hot.

picture overleaf

A great go-to recipe when anyone in the family is fighting off a cold. There's nothing like a bit of spice for unblocking a stuffy nose.

TOM YUM – SPICY PRAWN SOUP

Serves 2

500ml water
2 tbsp chilli paste
2 tbsp sliced lemongrass
3 tbsp sliced galangal
2 lime leaves, sliced
150ml fish sauce
150ml lime juice
380g large, uncooked prawns
10 button mushrooms, halved
4 tbsp evaporated milk
2 tbsp freshly chopped coriander

Pour the water into a saucepan, add the chilli paste, lemongrass, galangal, lime leaves, fish sauce and lime juice and bring to the boil.

Add the prawns, mushrooms and evaporated milk and cook for 2 minutes until the prawns are pink.

Divide between two bowls and garnish with the coriander to serve.

picture overleaf

FROM THE WATER

When I take Andy and the kids back to Thailand,
we love to visit the small fishing villages on the
coast. As well as the fun of being by the sea, we've
had some of our most memorable meals in small
harbour eateries with the freshest of seafood dishes
that appear simple but are rich in flavour.

This dish has a robust savoury flavour, unlike many classic Thai dishes that have a hint of sweetness. It's also fun as you have to unwrap it before you can enjoy it, like a present.

TURMERIC SEA BASS PARCELS

Serves 2

4 tbsp Stir-fry Sauce (see page 12)
2 tbsp light soy sauce
2 tbsp granulated sugar
½ tsp cracked black pepper
2 tbsp crushed garlic
1 tsp and a pinch of salt
2 tbsp crushed fresh turmeric
1 tbsp sliced lemongrass
10 Thai basil leaves
2 sea bass fillets, skin on
2 banana leaves, or greaseproof paper and foil
String to tie the parcels if using a banana leaf

For the stir-fried veg

15ml vegetable or rapeseed oil
1 pak choi, cut into 6 pieces, blanched
6 Tenderstem broccoli florets, blanched

Put the stir-fry sauce, light soy sauce, sugar, black pepper, crushed garlic, 1 teaspoon of salt, turmeric, lemongrass and Thai basil in a dish, mix together briefly, then add the sea bass fillets. Rub the marinade over each sea bass fillet, then wrap each one in a banana leaf or greaseproof paper with an outer layer of foil. Leave to marinate for 2 hours. If using banana leaf, tie the parcel with string.

Grill the sea bass, still wrapped in banana leaf or greaseproof paper and foil, in a flat frying pan or griddle pan over a medium to high heat for 4 minutes, turning to ensure the sea bass is evenly cooked.

Heat the oil in a wok and stir-fry the pak choi and broccoli for 2 minutes. Season with a pinch of salt.

Place the sea bass parcels on serving plates and arrange the stir-fried veg on the side.

Paneang is a less well-known Thai curry, which due to its vibrant red colour is often mistaken for its fiery red cousin. It tends to be thicker than a Thai red curry and richer and sweeter, with a nutty, rounded flavour.

SALMON PANEANG

Serves 2

2 tbsp self-raising flour

2 salmon fillets, skin on

95ml vegetable or rapeseed oil

400ml coconut milk

2 tbsp palm sugar (or soft brown sugar)

Pinch of salt

1 pak choi, cut into 6 pieces, blanched

6 Tenderstem broccoli florets, blanched

For the curry paste

6 large dried chillies

1 tsp cumin seeds

1 tsp coriander seeds

2 tbsp sliced lemongrass

2 tbsp chopped galangal

2 tsp crushed garlic

2 tsp diced red onion

2 tsp paprika

Scatter the flour over a plate and dust the salmon fillets in it, making sure they are completely coated.

Pour 30ml of the oil into a flat non-stick frying or griddle pan over a medium to high heat, add the salmon and pan-fryfor 6–7 minutes, turning

to ensure the salmon is evenly cooked. Once cooked, remove from the pan and set aside.

Put all the curry paste ingredients in a mortar and pound to a paste with the pestle. Alternatively, whizz together in a small food processor (see picture page 62).

Heat 50ml of the oil in a wok over medium to high heat, add the curry paste and cook for 2–3 minutes until it releases the oil from the sides; this cooking method helps to remove the rawness of the curry paste and also releases the flavour of the herbs.

Add the coconut milk, palm sugar and 1 teaspoon of salt and cook for a minute until mixed through and thickened.

Heat the remaining 15ml of oil in a separate wok and stir-fry the pak choi and broccoli for 2 minutes until cooked. Season with a pinch of salt.

Place the cooked salmon on serving plates, arrange the stir-fried veg on the side and top with the sauce .

picture on previous page.

A great dish to spoil your friends with when cooking for a crowd, or you can double the quantities below to serve 4 people. Simple but indulgent, it shows off Thailand's abundance of seafood with gentle spice and a sweet hint of coconut milk.

FISHING VILLAGE

Serves 2

50ml vegetable or rapeseed oil

2 tbsp crushed red chilli

2 tbsp crushed garlic

200g seafood mix, including prawns,
  squid and mussels

4 tbsp Stir-fry Sauce (see page 12)

2 tsp light soy sauce

150ml coconut milk

10 Thai basil leaves

For the curry paste

6 large dried chillies

2 tbsp chopped galangal

2 tsp crushed garlic

2 tbsp sliced lemongrass

1 tsp cumin seeds

1 tsp coriander seeds

2 tsp diced red onion

2 tsp paprika

Put all the curry paste ingredients in a mortar and pound to a paste with the pestle. Alternatively, whizz together in a small food processor.

Heat the oil in a wok over medium to high heat, add the crushed chilli and garlic and cook for a minute, then add the curry paste and cook for 2–3 minutes until it releases the oil from the sides; this cooking method helps to remove the rawness of the curry paste and also releases the flavour of the herbs.

Add all the seafood, stir-fry sauce and light soy sauce and stir-fry for 2 minutes.

Finally, add the coconut milk and basil and cook for a further minute.

Remove from the heat, divide into two equal portions and serve with coconut rice (see page 140).

picture overleaf

A stir-fry that is all about the heat – from its name, which is describing the sizzling sound as the fresh seafood makes contact with the hot wok, to that warming chilli kick. Enjoy this fiery, fresh seafood stir-fry and imagine being in a small fishing village in the hot sun.

SEAFOOD PAD CHA

Serves 2

50ml vegetable or rapeseed oil

2 tsp crushed red chilli

2 tbsp crushed garlic

200g seafood mix, including prawns,
     squid and mussels

2 tbsp Stir-fry Sauce (see page 12)

2 tbsp light soy sauce

2 tbsp sliced lemongrass

1 small courgette, sliced

10 fine green beans, sliced

10 Thai basil leaves

For the curry paste

6 large dried chillies

2 tbsp chopped galangal

2 tsp crushed garlic

2 tbsp sliced lemongrass

1 tsp cumin seeds

1 tsp coriander seeds

2 tsp diced red onion

2 tsp paprika

Put all the curry paste ingredients in a mortar and pound to a paste with the pestle. Alternatively, whizz together in a small food processor.

Heat the oil in a wok over medium to high heat, add the crushed chilli and garlic and cook for a minute, then add the curry paste and cook for 2–3 minutes until it releases the oil from the sides; this cooking method helps to remove the rawness of the curry paste and also releases the flavour of the herbs.

Add all the seafood, stir-fry sauce and light soy sauce and stir-fry for 2 minutes.

Finally, add the lemongrass, courgette, green beans and Thai basil and cook for 2 minutes.

Divide between two plates and serve with coconut rice (see page 140).

Simple but divine. This may not be the prettiest dish, because the sauce is a humble green, but perhaps because of this, the sheer depth of flavour always comes as a bit of a surprise.

HAKE GREEN GODDESS

Serves 2

2 hake fillets, skin on
2 tbsp self-raising flour
75ml vegetable or rapeseed oil
6 tbsp coconut milk
2 tbsp light soy sauce
1 pak choi, sliced and blanched
8 Tenderstem broccoli florets, blanched
A handful of green beans, sliced and blanched
Pinch of salt

For the curry paste
20g green chillies, roughly chopped
½ green pepper, deseeded and roughly sliced
2 sprigs of fresh coriander
10 fresh mint leaves
2 tbsp lime juice
1 tsp cumin seeds
1 tsp coriander seeds

Coat the hake fillets in flour, making sure they are completely covered.

Heat 30ml of the oil in a flat frying or griddle pan over a medium to high heat and cook the hake, skin side down, 2 minutes, then turn over and cook for a further for 2 minutes until the fish is cooked through.

Put all the curry paste ingredients in a mortar and pound to a paste with the pestle. Alternatively, whizz together in a small food processor.

Heat 30ml of the oil in a wok over medium to high heat, add the curry paste and cook for 2–3 minutes until it releases the oil to remove the rawness of the curry paste and release the flavour of the herbs. Add the coconut milk and soy sauce and cook for 1 minute until thoroughly mixed.

Heat the remaining 15ml oil in a separate wok and stir-fry the pak choi, broccoli and green beans for 2 minutes. Season with a pinch of salt.

Arrange the hake and veg on serving plates and top the hake with the green sauce.

Sea bass has the kind of generous, accommodating flavour that works as the perfect backdrop to bold, fresh ingredients like lime juice, garlic, ginger and chilli – perfect for Thai dishes.

SUNNY DAY SEA BASS

Serves 2

2 sea bass fillets, skin on

200g mixed mushrooms, such as shiitake, oyster and button, sliced

Thumb-sized piece of fresh ginger, peeled and thinly sliced into matchsticks

1 shallot, sliced

For the sauce

1 red chilli, roughly chopped

4 tbsp granulated sugar

2 garlic cloves

4 sprigs of fresh coriander

150ml lime juice

120ml fish sauce

Put all the sauce ingredients in a small food processor and blend to a coarse paste.

Boil the sea bass in a pan of hot water for 2 minutes until cooked. Drain.

In a separate pan, boil the mixed mushrooms in water for 2 minutes. Drain.

Place the sea bass fillets on serving plates alongside the cooked mushrooms. Coat the cooked sea bass with the sauce and garnish with the sliced ginger and shallot.

FROM THE LAND

We tend to eat a lot of chicken and pork in Thailand, but beef is also becoming popular, and our Crying Beef dish (on page 76) is always a crowd-pleaser, served on a sizzling skillet and running with juices.

Our version of the classic Thai dish, which goes by many different names, but is often known as Weeping Tiger, although the only sound you'll hear while cooking this dish is the delicious sizzle of beef.

CRYING BEEF

Serves 2

1 tsp salt

2 pinches of cracked black pepper

1 tsp granulated sugar

2 tbsp Stir-fry Sauce (see page 12)

2 sirloin steaks, weighing about 180g each

15ml vegetable or rapeseed oil

10 fine green beans, halved

½ red onion, sliced

½ white onion, sliced

Handful of iceberg lettuce leaves

8 cherry tomatoes, halved

For the dipping sauce

2 tbsp tamarind juice

2 tsp lime juice

2 tbsp fish sauce

1 tsp chilli flakes, crushed in a pestle and mortar

½ tsp granulated sugar

Put the salt, pepper, sugar and stir-fry sauce in a dish and mix together. Add the steaks and leave to marinate for 2 hours.

To make the dipping sauce, put all the ingredients in a bowl and mix together. Set aside.

Remove the steaks from the marinade and transfer to a hot flat frying or griddle pan and cook – for Rare: 1½ minutes per side; Medium rare: 2 minutes per side; Medium: about 2¼ minutes per side; Well-done: Cook for about 4–5 minutes each side, depending on thickness. Remove from the pan and set aside to rest.

Heat the oil in a wok or deep saucepan over a medium to high heat and sauté the beans, red and white onion for about 4 minutes.

Slice the steak, place the sautéed veg on the side along with the dipping sauce in a bowl or dip pot. Serve with the lettuce and cherry tomatoes on the side.

This is the Christmas version of our popular Sticky Chicken dish with the addition of some delicious wintery ingredients, like chestnuts and prunes.

FESTIVE STICKY CHICKEN

Serves 2

150g self-raising flour

3 eggs

30ml water

Pinch of salt

1 tsp ground white pepper

300g chicken breast, sliced

780ml vegetable or rapeseed oil

50g whole prunes

50g water chestnuts, halved

50g whole chestnuts

1 spring onion, finely sliced

2 tbsp sliced red chilli

1 tsp toasted sesame seeds

For the sauce

6 tbsp Stir-fry Sauce (see page 12)

2 tsp toasted sesame oil

4 tbsp water

30g ready-made chilli garlic sauce
   (we like Lee Kum Kee)

To make the sauce, put all the ingredients in a bowl and mix together. Set aside.

Whisk the flour, eggs, water, salt and white pepper together in a bowl. Dip the chicken slices in the mixture, making sure they are completely coated.

Pour 750ml of the oil into a wok over a medium to high heat and deep-fry the chicken for 3 minutes until golden brown and crispy.

Pour the remaining 30ml oil into a separate wok over a medium to high heat, then add the sauce and cook for 1 minute. Add the deep-fried chicken, prunes, water chestnuts and chestnuts and quickly stir-fry for a minute until evenly coated in the sauce.

Transfer the sticky chicken to serving plates, garnish with the sliced spring onion and red chilli and scatter over the toasted sesame seeds to serve.

picture previous page

This is the Thai version of fast food because it's so quick and easy to make and probably the first thing we think of when grabbing a quick lunch from a street-food vendor during the working week.

CHICKEN GRA PAO WITH FRIED EGGS

Serves 2

100ml vegetable or rapeseed oil
2 eggs
2 tbsp crushed garlic
2 tbsp crushed chilli
300g chicken breast, sliced
6 tbsp Stir-fry Sauce (see page 12)
1 tbsp light soy sauce
2 pinches of cracked black pepper
½ red pepper, deseeded and sliced
½ green pepper, deseeded and sliced
10 fine green beans, halved
10 Thai basil leaves

Pour the oil into a wok over a medium to high heat, crack in the eggs and fry sunny side up. Remove the eggs from the wok and set aside.

Using the same oil in the wok, add the crushed garlic and chilli and sauté for a minute over a medium to high heat to release the flavour.

Add the sliced chicken breast and cook for 2 minutes. Next, add the stir-fry sauce, light soy sauce and black pepper and stir briefly, then add the red and green pepper, beans and Thai basil and cook for a further 2 minutes.

Remove from the heat and divide between two bowls or plates and top each with a fried egg. Serve with coconut rice (see page 140).

picture overleaf

A fiery crowd-pleaser, with the heat and flavour of red chillies and garlic bursting through the fresh vegetables. For me this epitomises Thai cooking, with fresh ingredients thrown into a hot wok to seal in all the flavour and goodness.

VEGETARIAN GRA PAO v

Serves 2

100ml vegetable or rapeseed oil

2 eggs

2 tbsp crushed chilli

2 tbsp crushed garlic

60g carrots, peeled and cut into batons

60g courgette, sliced

6 broccoli florets, halved

10 fine green beans, halved

6 tbsp Stir-fry Sauce (see page 12)

2 tbsp light soy sauce

2 pinches of cracked black pepper

10 holy basil leaves

Pour the oil into a wok over a medium to high heat, crack in the eggs and fry sunny side up. Remove the eggs from the wok and set aside.

Using the same oil in the wok, add the crushed chilli and garlic and sauté for a minute over a medium to high heat to release the flavour.

Add all the vegetables, stir-fry sauce, light soy sauce, black pepper and holy basil and cook for a further 2 minutes.

Remove from the heat and divide between two bowls or plates, then top each with a fried egg. Serve with coconut rice (see page 140).

For a delicious vegan-friendly version of the vegetarian Gran Pao omit the eggs.

VEGAN GRA PAO VG

Serves 2

30ml vegetable or rapeseed oil

2 tbsp crushed chilli

2 tbsp crushed garlic

60g carrots, peeled and cut into batons

60g courgette, sliced

6 broccoli florets, halved

10 fine green beans, halved

60ml Stir-fry Sauce (see page 12)

2 tbsp light soy sauce

2 pinches of cracked black pepper

10 holy basil leaves

Pour the oil into a wok over medium to high heat, add the crushed chilli and garlic and sauté for a minute to release the flavour.

Add all the vegetables, Stir-fry Sauce, light soy sauce, black pepper and holy basil and cook for a further 2 minutes.

Divide between two plates or bowls and serve with coconut rice (see page 140).

picture previous page

The trick here to achieving the pleasing tenderness of the pork is in the slow cooking. Well worth the time for the sublime textures and flavours.

CHUBBY CHEEK PORK

Serves 2

750ml water

320g pork cheeks

1 cinnamon stick

1 star anise

1 tsp salt

1 tsp granulated sugar, plus extra to serve

1 tsp cracked black pepper, plus more to serve

2 tbsp vegetable or rapeseed oil

2 tbsp crushed garlic

300ml just-boiled water

150ml Stir-fry Sauce (see page 12)

6 tbsp granulated sugar

2 tbsp light soy sauce

6 broccoli florets

60g carrots, peeled and cut into batons

10 sugar snap peas

To cook the pork cheeks, pour the water into a deep saucepan, then add the pork cheeks, cinnamon stick, star anise, salt, sugar and pepper and cook over a low heat for 2 hours until the pork cheeks are soft and tender.

Pour the oil into a wok over a medium to high heat, then add the garlic and sauté for a minute.

Add the hot water, stir-fry sauce, sugar and light soy sauce and cook for 2 minutes until the sauce thickens.

Add the pork cheeks and mix well to properly coat them in sauce. Finally, add the broccoli, carrots and sugar snap peas and cook for a further 2 minutes until all the veg is cooked.

Divide between two bowls, sprinkle with cracked black pepper and serve with coconut rice (see page 140).

The butternut squash halves create the perfect receptacles for all the flavourful veggie goodness in this recipe. In our book, there's no excuse for plant-based food to ever lack taste or texture.

BUTTERNUT BOAT VG

Serves 2

1 butternut squash, halved lengthways, seeds removed

30ml vegetable or rapeseed oil

150ml coconut milk

1 small courgette, sliced

A handful of fine green beans, sliced

20g carrots, peeled and diced

6 broccoli florets, sliced

For the curry paste

2 medium green chillies, roughly chopped

½ green pepper, deseeded and roughly sliced

2 sprigs of fresh coriander

10 fresh mint leaves

2 tbsp lime juice

1 tsp cumin seeds

1 tsp coriander seeds

50ml Stir-fry Sauce (see page 12)

1 tbsp granulated sugar

1 tsp sliced lemongrass

Bring a large saucepan of water to the boil, add the butternut squash halves and cook until tender. Remove from the pan and scoop out the flesh in chunks. Reserve the flesh and the scooped-out halves.

Put all the curry paste ingredients in a food processor or blender and blend to smooth paste.

Pour the oil into a wok or pan over a medium to high heat, add the curry paste and cook for 2–3 minutes until it releases the oil from the sides; this cooking method helps to remove the rawness of the curry paste and also releases the flavour of the herbs.

Add the coconut milk and cook for 1 minute until thoroughly mixed with the curry paste, then add the courgette, green beans, carrots, broccoli and butternut squash flesh and simmer for 2 minutes.

Divide the sauce and veggies between the two butternut halves and serve.

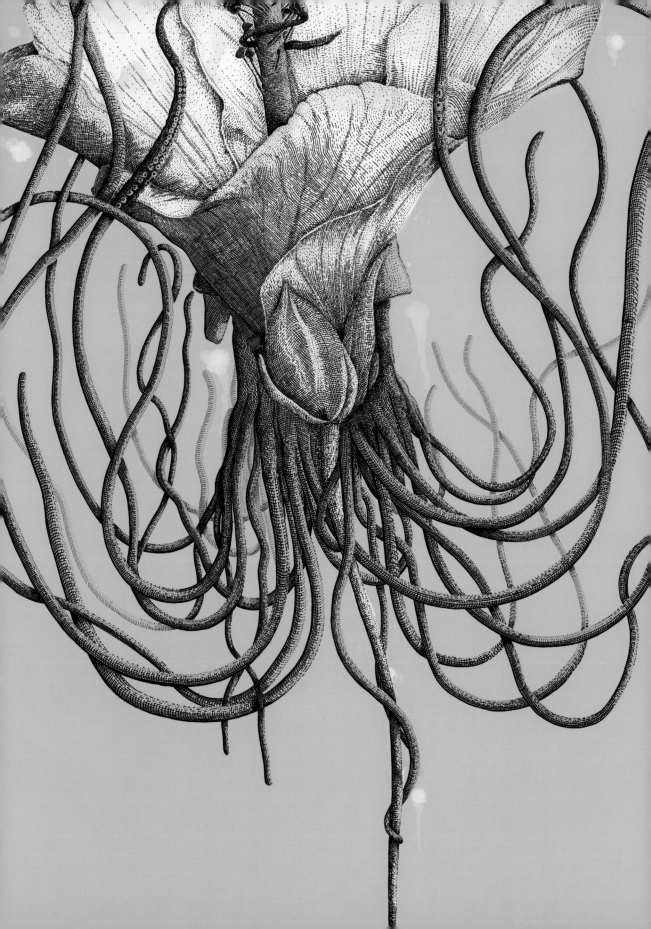

CURRIES

You really fall in love with Thai curries when you
have the time to grind up a curry paste in a pestle
and mortar, filling your kitchen with the unique
fragrance of beautiful herbs and spices like
lemongrass, galangal, garlic and ginger (I could
add many more to the list). That's when you
really fall in love with a Thai curry!

People often make the mistake of thinking that Thai red curry is the hottest – maybe due to its fiery red colour – but a Thai green curry is definitely the spiciest! Chicken on the bone is a favourite protein for green curry across Thailand and in the northern area we tend to enjoy it with noodles rather than rice.

THAI GREEN CURRY

Serves 2

50ml vegetable or rapeseed oil
500ml coconut milk
200g chicken breast or beef steak, thinly
   sliced, or 200g large uncooked prawns
2 tbsp palm sugar (or soft brown sugar)
2 tsp salt
2 tsp light soy sauce
100ml water
15g courgette, sliced
½ red, green or yellow pepper, deseeded
   and sliced
20g bamboo shoots
15g fine green beans, halved
10 Thai basil leaves
4 lime leaves

For the curry paste
8 green bird's eye chillies
2 long green chillies
15g lemongrass, sliced
15g galangal, sliced
6 garlic cloves
1 tsp coriander seeds
2 tbsp diced red onion
4 lime leaves
8 sweet basil leaves
1 tsp fresh or ground turmeric

Put all the curry paste ingredients in a mortar and pound to a paste with the pestle. Alternatively, whizz together in a small food processor.

Pour the oil into a wok over a medium to high heat, add the curry paste and cook for 3–4 minutes until it releases the oil from the sides; this cooking method helps to remove the rawness of the curry paste and also releases the flavour of the herbs.

Add the coconut milk, your protein of choice, sugar, salt, soy sauce and water and bring to the boil. Then add all the vegetables, Thai basil and lime leaves cook for 2–3 minutes.

Divide between two plates or bowls and serve with coconut rice (see page 140).

A homemade curry paste will infuse your curry with a depth and richness of flavour that no one could mistake for shop-bought!

THAI RED CURRY WITH VEGETABLES

Serves 2

50ml vegetable or rapeseed cooking oil

500ml coconut milk

200g chicken breast or beef steak, thinly sliced, or 200g large uncooked prawns (optional)

100ml water

2 tbsp palm sugar (or soft brown sugar)

2 tsp salt

2 tsp light soy sauce

20g bamboo shoots

20g courgette, sliced

20g carrot, peeled and cut into batons

15g fine green beans, halved

10 Thai basil leaves

4 lime leaves

For the curry paste

6 large dried chillies

2 tbsp chopped galangal

2 tsp crushed garlic

2 tbsp sliced lemongrass

1 tsp cumin seeds

1 tsp coriander seeds

2 tsp diced red onion

2 tsp paprika

Put all the curry paste ingredients in a mortar and pound to a paste with the pestle. Alternatively, whizz together in a small food processor.

Heat the oil in a wok over medium to high heat, add the curry paste and cook for 3–4 minutes until it releases the oil from the sides; this cooking method helps to remove the rawness of the curry paste and also releases the flavour of the herbs.

Pour in the coconut milk, your choice of chicken, beef or prawns (if using), the sugar, salt and soy sauce and bring it to a boil.

Next, add all the vegetables, basil and lime leaves and cook for a further 2 minutes.

Divide between two plates or bowls and serve with coconut rice (see page 140).

picture previous page

A dish that demands a hearty appetite, absolutely crammed with fish and seafood. In reality, it's the bounty straight off the fishing boats but it's such a showstopper dish we gave it a regal name!

ROYAL FISHING BOAT CURRY

Serves 2

6 tbsp self-raising flour
2 skinless salmon fillets
100ml vegetable or rapeseed oil
600ml coconut milk
2 tsp mild curry powder
2 tsp ground turmeric
2 tbsp light soy sauce
2 tsp salt
6 tbsp palm sugar (or soft brown)
200g seafood mix, including squid,
    prawns and mussels
4 pearl onions
4 carrots, peeled and diced

For the curry paste
1 red chilli, sliced
2 dried red chillies
1 tsp fresh turmeric
20g sliced red onions
2 tsp sliced lemongrass
2 tsp cracked black pepper

Scatter the flour over a plate and dust the salmon fillets in it, making sure they are completely coated.

Put all the curry paste ingredients in a mortar and pound to a paste with the pestle. Alternatively, whizz together in a small food processor.

Pour half the oil into a flat non-stick frying or griddle pan over a medium to high heat, add the salmon fillets and pan-fry for 6–7 minutes turning to ensure the salmon is evenly cooked. Remove from the pan and set aside.

Pour the remaining oil into a clean wok over a medium to high heat, add the curry paste and cook for 2–3 minutes until it releases the oil from the sides; this cooking method helps to remove the rawness of the curry paste and also releases the flavour of the herbs.

Add the coconut milk, curry powder, ground turmeric, soy sauce, salt and sugar and bring to a simmer, then add all the seafood, pearl onions and carrots and stir through. Cook for 2 more minutes.

Place the cooked salmon fillets in the centre of two plates and pour the sauce on and around the salmon to serve.

picture overleaf

Jungle curry, or *Kaeng Pa*, apparently got its name because it was cooked by deer and boar hunters in the Thai jungles. There's no coconut milk but it's distinctively Thai in flavour.

KAENG PA – TROPICAL JUNGLE CURRY

Serves 2

500ml water
200g chicken breast or beef steak, thinly sliced, or 200g large uncooked prawns
30g bamboo shoots, sliced
15g courgette, sliced
6 fine green beans, halved
6 baby corn, halved
4 tbsp Stir-fry Sauce (see page 12)
1 tsp salt
2 tsp light soy sauce
2 lime leaves
10 Thai basil leaves

For the curry paste
4 dried large chillies
¼ sliced red chilli
2 tbsp crushed garlic
2 tbsp diced red onion
2 tsp sliced lemongrass

Put all the curry paste ingredients in a mortar and pound to a paste with the pestle. Alternatively, whizz together in a small food processor.

Pour the water into a wok over a medium to high heat, add the curry paste and cook for 2 minutes. Add the raw chicken, beef or prawns, bamboo shoots, courgette, fine beans and baby corn and cook for a further 2 minutes. Finally, add the stir-fry sauce, salt, soy sauce, lime leaves and Thai basil and cook for a final minute.

Divide between two plates or bowls and serve with coconut rice (see page 140).

Massaman is a fusion dish with a story –
it was introduced to the central Thai court
by Persian traders in the seventeenth
century. We love how it blends spices from
the Indian subcontinent such as cardamom
and star anise with the classic Thai flavours
of galangal and lemongrass.

LAMB SHANK MASSAMAN

Serves 2

2 lamb shanks

2 litres water

3 star anise

8 green cardamom pods

2 bay leaves

1 tbsp salt, plus 4 tsp

6 new potatoes

4 carrots, cubed

50ml vegetable or rapeseed oil

1 cinnamon stick

6 tbsp tamarind juice

500ml coconut milk

4 tbsp palm sugar (or soft brown sugar)

For the curry paste

6 large dried chillies

2 tsp sliced lemongrass

2 tsp sliced galangal

2 tsp crushed garlic

Put the lamb shanks in a large casserole
dish, pour over the measured water and
add a star anise, half the green cardamom
pods, the bay leaves and 1 tablespoon of
salt. Cover with a lid and cook over a low
heat for 2–3 hours until soft and tender.

Meanwhile, bring the saucepan of water to
a boil, add the new potatoes and cook for
10 minutes, adding the carrots for the final
3–4 minutes of cooking.

Put all the curry paste ingredients in a
mortar and pound to a paste with the pestle.
Alternatively, whizz together in a small
food processor.

Pour the oil into a wok over a medium to
high heat, add the cinnamon stick, remaining
star anise and cardamom pods and cook for
a minute to release the flavour. Now add the
curry paste and cook for 2 minutes until it
releases the oil from the sides.

Add the 4 teaspoons of salt, tamarind juice, coconut milk and sugar and cook for 5 minutes.

Add the cooked lamb shanks, carrots and potatoes to the wok and cook for 2 minutes.

Divide between two bowls and serve with coconut rice (see page 140).

picture overleaf

A warming vegan feast in a bowl with butternut squash, carrots and courgettes, perfect for the colder months. The tamarind gives it a real flavour lift alongside a little heat from the chillies.

WINTER WARMER CURRY VG

Serves 2

50ml vegetable or rapeseed oil
500ml coconut milk
6 tbsp palm sugar (or soft brown sugar)
2 tsp salt
6 tbsp tamarind juice
140g cooked butternut squash, diced
4 baby onions
30g carrots, peeled and cut into batons
30g courgette, sliced

For the curry paste
¼ red chilli, sliced
4 dried chillies
2 tsp sliced lemongrass
2 tsp crushed garlic
1 tsp cumin seeds
1 tsp coriander seeds

Put all the curry paste ingredients in a mortar and pound to a paste with the pestle. Alternatively, whizz together in a small food processor.

Pour the oil into a wok over a medium to high heat, add the curry paste and cook for 2–3 minutes until it releases the oil from the sides; this cooking method helps to remove the rawness of the curry paste and also releases the flavour of the herbs.

Add the coconut milk, sugar, salt and tamarind juice and bring to the boil. Add all the vegetables, reduce the heat and simmer for 2 minutes until the vegetables are cooked.

Divide between two bowls and serve with coconut rice (see page 140).

There's real love and effort that goes into cooking this dish properly, but the flavour of the sauce – sweet and rich – works beautifully with the crispy-skinned duck, making it a long-time favourite in our restaurants.

RISING STAR
RED DUCK CURRY

Serves 2

2 duck breasts
30ml vegetable or rapeseed oil
500ml coconut milk
2 tsp salt
6 tbsp palm sugar (or soft brown sugar)
10 Thai basil leaves
10 pineapple chunks
6 green grapes
4 cherry tomatoes

For the curry paste
2 tsp diced red onion
¼ red chilli, sliced
4 dried chillies
2 tsp crushed garlic
2 tsp sliced lemongrass
2 tbsp freshly chopped coriander
1 tsp cumin seeds

Place the duck breasts, skin side down, on a griddle pan over a medium to high heat and cook for 6 minutes to render the fat. Turn the duck breasts over and cook for a further 4 minutes. Remove from the pan and leave to rest for 10 minutes.

Put all the curry paste ingredients in a mortar and pound to a paste with the pestle. Alternatively, whizz together in a small food processor.

Pour the oil into a wok over a medium to high heat, add the curry paste and cook for 2–3 minutes until it releases the oil from the sides; this cooking method helps to remove the rawness of the curry paste and also releases the flavour of the herbs.

Add the coconut milk, salt, sugar and Thai basil and bring to a simmer until the sugar dissolves, then add the pineapple, green grapes and tomatoes and cook for a further minute.

Slice the duck breasts and divide between two plates, pour over the sauce to cover and serve with coconut rice (see page 140).

A friend of ours made this dish when we visited her in Kanchanaburi. She didn't hold back on the spiciness but we've toned the heat down a little for this recipe so the magical blend of flavours can be enjoyed without setting your teeth on fire!

KHWAE RIVER CURRY

Serves 2

50ml vegetable or rapeseed oil

240g pork collar, thinly sliced

500ml coconut milk

1 tsp salt

2 tbsp granulated sugar

4 green grapes

1 green chilli, chopped

10 Thai basil leaves

2 pieces of roti, to serve

For the curry paste

2 dried red chillies

2 slices of red chilli

2 tsp crushed garlic

2 tsp diced red onion

2 tsp sliced lemongrass

1 tsp cumin seeds

1 tsp coriander seeds

Put all the curry paste ingredients in a mortar and pound to a paste with the pestle. Alternatively, whizz together in a small food processor.

Pour the oil into a wok over a medium to high heat, add the curry paste and cook for 2–3 minutes until it releases the oil from the sides; this cooking method helps to remove the rawness of the curry paste and also releases the flavour of the herbs.

Add the sliced pork collar and cook for 2 minutes. Now add the coconut milk, salt, sugar, green grapes, green chilli and Thai basil and simmer for 2 minutes.

Heat the roti in a flat non-stick frying pan for 2 minutes on each side.

Serve the pork curry with the roti alongside. (For homemade roti see page 146).

STIR-FRIES

A flaming wok, a dash of oil and the freshest
of ingredients thrown in and cooked quickly
to release the flavour and preserve the nutrients
of the vegetables and proteins – these simple
stir-fries are the essence of Thai cooking.

A great dish for when you need to rustle up something quick and delicious after a long day.

HOME
COMFORT BEEF

Serves 2

50ml vegetable or rapeseed cooking oil

2 tbsp crushed garlic

2 tbsp crushed chilli

300g beef mince

6 tbsp Stir-fry Sauce (see page 12)

2 tbsp light soy sauce

2 pinches of granulated sugar

2 pinches of freshly ground black pepper

20 fine green beans, cut into halves

40g sugar snaps

10 Thai sweet basil leaves

1 red chilli, sliced

Pour the oil into a wok over a medium to high heat.

Add the crushed garlic and chilli and sauté for a minute.

Add the mince and stir-fry until browned.

Next, add the stir-fry sauce, light soy sauce, sugar, and pepper followed by the fine beans, sugar snaps, basil and sliced red chilli and cook for a further 2 minutes.

Divide between two serving bowls or plates and serve with coconut rice (see page 140).

The lovely golden hue of this stir-fry comes from fresh and ground turmeric, which can be quite a bitter spice but finds perfect balance with the chicken, bamboo shoots and coconut milk here.

GOLDEN BAMBOO & CHICKEN STIR-FRY

Serves 2

50ml vegetable or rapeseed oil

200g chicken breast, sliced

300ml coconut milk

100g bamboo shoots

30g courgette, sliced

2 tsp salt

2 tbsp white sugar

2 tbsp light soy sauce

2 tsp ground turmeric

10 Thai basil leaves

4 lime leaves, finely sliced

For the curry paste

4 red chillies, roughly chopped

2 tsp sliced lemongrass

2 tsp fresh turmeric, peeled and
   roughly chopped

1 tsp black peppercorns

Put all the curry paste ingredients in a mortar and pound to a paste with the pestle. Alternatively, whizz together in a small food processor.

Heat the oil in a wok over a medium to high heat, then add the curry paste and cook for 2–3 minutes until it releases the oil from the sides; this cooking method helps to remove the rawness of the curry paste and also releases the flavour of the herbs.

Add the chicken and cook for 2 minutes, then pour in the coconut milk. Add the bamboo shoots, courgette, salt, sugar, soy sauce and ground turmeric and cook for a further 2 minutes.

Add the Thai basil and sliced lime leaves and toss through, then remove from heat and divide between two plates or bowls to serve.

We created this simple but ingredient-rich dish as a Veganuary special a few years back. There's such a variety of vegetables and herbs available now, each bringing their own unique flavour and texture, that we strongly believe there's no excuse for bland vegan dishes!

THE WONDER WOK VG

Serves 2

4 tbsp vegetable or rapeseed oil
150g Quorn pieces
100g sugar snap peas
10 water chestnuts, sliced
10 chestnuts
½ red pepper, sliced
½ green pepper, sliced
½ white onion, sliced
4 tbsp light soy sauce
4 tbsp hoisin sauce
4 tbsp sriracha sauce
2 tsp white sugar

Pour the oil into a wok over a medium to high heat, then add the Quorn, sugar snap peas, water chestnuts, whole chestnuts, peppers and onion and cook for 5 minutes. Pour in the soy, hoisin and sriracha sauces along with the sugar and cook for a final minute.

Divide between two bowls and serve.

The cashews really lift the flavour and texture of this stir-fry to another level, adding their distinctive hint of sweetness and even a certain creaminess, too.

WHOLESOME CASHEW STIR-FRY VG

Serves 2

4 tbsp vegetable or rapeseed oil

2 tsp crushed garlic

6 broccoli florets, halved

1 red or green pepper, deseeded and sliced

Handful of fine green beans, halved

½ onion, sliced

½ courgette, sliced

50ml cold water

4 tbsp cashew nuts

3 tbsp light soy sauce

2 tbsp chilli garlic sauce (we like Lee Kum Kee)

2 tbsp sriracha sauce

Pour the oil into a wok over a medium to high heat, then add the crushed garlic and stir-fry for a minute to release the flavour and remove the rawness of the garlic. Stir in all the vegetables and water and allow the veg to cook for a minute, then add the cashew nuts and all three sauces and continue to cook for a final minute.

Divide between two bowls and serve.

NOODLES, RICE & SIDES

Thai meals are all about the balance of flavour
and texture – dampening the fire of a particularly
hot curry with fragrant rice and rotis or enhancing
a sizzling pork or chicken dish with the fresh
green crunch of vegetables.

Pad Thai may well be one of the best-known Thai dishes, but we bet you didn't know that it was created as a national dish in 1938 to help combat a rice shortage.

GIGGLING PAD THAI

Serves 2

300ml vegetable or rapeseed oil, plus 2 tbsp

150g firm tofu, cubed

2 eggs, beaten

½ small red onion, sliced

200g chicken breast, sliced, or 200g
    large uncooked prawns

6 broccoli florets, halved

80g carrots, peeled and cut into batons

300g rice noodles, cooked according to
    packet instructions

2 small handfuls of beansprouts

2 tbsp chopped chives or spring onions

2 tbsp unsalted roasted peanuts, crushed

2 lime wedges

For the Pad Thai sauce

150ml tamarind juice

200g palm sugar (or soft brown sugar)

2 pinches of salt

Mix all the Pad Thai sauce ingredients together in a mixing bowl and set aside.

Pour the 300ml oil into a wok or deep saucepan over a medium-high heat and deep-fry the tofu until golden brown. Remove from the wok and set aside.

Heat the remaining 2 tablespoons of oil in a separate wok over a medium to high heat, add the eggs and cook through for 1 minute. Then add the red onion and chicken or prawns and cook for 2 minutes until the onion has softened and the chicken is cooked through.

Add the broccoli, carrots and cooked tofu and stir-fry for 2 minutes until the veg is cooked.

Add the cooked rice noodles along with 180ml of the Pad Thai sauce and stir-fry for 1 minute, then add the beansprouts and chives (or spring onions) and mix through.

Divide between two plates or bowls, scatter over the crushed peanuts and serve each with a lime wedge alongside.

Our vegan Pad Thai really is the ultimate comfort dish, with rich stir-fry flavours, satisfying noodles and fresh vegetables.

VEGAN PAD THAI vg

Serves 2

300ml vegetable or rapeseed oil, plus 2 tbsp
150g firm tofu, cubed
½ small red onion, sliced
6 broccoli florets, halved
80g carrots, peeled and cut into batons
300g rice noodles, cooked according
    to packet instructions
¼ sweetheart cabbage, sliced
2 small handfuls of beansprouts
2 tbsp chopped chives or spring onions
2 tbsp unsalted roasted peanuts, crushed
2 lime wedges

For the Pad Thai sauce
150ml tamarind juice
200g palm sugar (or soft brown sugar)
2 pinches of salt

Mix all the Pad Thai sauce ingredients together in a mixing bowl and set aside.

Pour the 300ml of oil into a wok or deep saucepan over a medium to high heat and deep-fry the tofu until golden brown. Remove from the wok and set aside.

Pour the remaining 2 tablespoons of oil into a separate wok over a medium to high heat, then add the red onion and fry for a few minutes until softened. Add the broccoli, carrots and cooked tofu and stir-fry for 2 minutes until the veg is cooked. Add the cooked rice noodles and 180ml of the Pad Thai sauce and stir-fry for 1 minute, then add the beansprouts and chives (or spring onions) and mix through.

Divide between two plates or bowls, scatter over the crushed peanuts and serve with a lime wedge alongside.

picture previous page

The gorgeous deep-red colour is natural as these noodles are made from beetroot. Our experience of a meal always begins with our eyes and the beauty of these noodles brings an immediate happy anticipation.

RUBY NOODLES WITH BEANSPROUTS VG

Serves 2

4 tbsp vegetable or rapeseed oil

2 tsp crushed garlic

1 handful of sliced sweetheart cabbage

Handful of fine green beans, halved

150g ruby noodles, soaked
   in hot water for 15 minutes, then drained

2 tbsp light soy sauce

2 tsp granulated sugar

2 tbsp sriracha sauce

2 handfuls of beansprouts

2 spring onions, cut into 3cm batons

Pour the oil into a wok over a medium to high heat, add the garlic and cook for 30 seconds. Add the cabbage, beans, soaked noodles and mix briefly, then add the soy sauce, sugar and sriracha sauce and cook for a minute. Add the beansprouts and spring onions and cook for a final minute until all the ingredients are thoroughly mixed.

Divide between two bowls or plates and serve.

picture overleaf

Pad Kee Mao is often known as Drunken Noodles – perhaps because people end up drinking a little more than planned to put out the spicy fire in their mouths! Our version has a gentler heat and features gorgeous black charcoal noodles.

PAD KEE MAO – DRUNKEN CHARCOAL NOODLES VG

Serves 1

4 tbsp vegetable or rapeseed oil

2 tsp crushed garlic

2 tsp crushed red chilli

1 handful of sliced sweetheart cabbage

50g carrots, peeled and cut into batons

6 broccoli florets, halved

Handful of fine green beans, halved

150g charcoal noodles, soaked in hot water
    for 15 minutes, then drained

2 tbsp light soy sauce

4 tbsp Stir-fry Sauce (see page 12)

Pour the oil into a wok over a medium to high heat, add the crushed garlic and chilli and stir-fry for 30 seconds. Add the cabbage, carrots, broccoli and beans and stir-fry for 1 minute. Finally, add the charcoal noodles along with the soy sauce and stir-fry sauce and continue cooking for 1 minute until all the ingredients are thoroughly mixed.

Dish out on to a plate and serve immediately.

Super versatile, this is a perfect side for any meal, or you could increase the quantities for a quick and easy light lunch or dinner.

STIR-FRIED NOODLES WITH BEANSPROUTS VG

Serves 2

4 tbsp vegetable or rapeseed oil

300g rice noodles, cooked according to packet instructions

4 tbsp Stir-fry Sauce (see page 12)

2 tbsp light soy sauce

1 tsp cracked black pepper

50g carrots, peeled and cut into batons

2 handfuls of beansprouts

2 springs onion, cut into batons

Pour the oil into a wok over a medium to high heat, add the rice noodles and a splash of hot water and stir-fry for a minute, ensuring the rice noodles do not stick to the pan and break.

Add the stir-fry sauce, soy sauce, black pepper and carrots and continue cooking for a minute until all the ingredients are coated in the sauce. Finally, add the beansprouts and spring onions and cook for a final minute.

Transfer to a serving bowl.

A Thai staple but little known in the UK, morning glory is a long-stemmed leafy green that stir-fries beautifully and works so well with a little chilli spice.

MORNING GLORY VG

Serves 2

2 tbsp rapeseed oil

200g morning glory, cut into 5cm pieces

1 clove of garlic, crushed

1 red chilli, sliced

1 tbsp soya bean paste

2 tbsp Stir-fry Sauce (page 12)

3 tbsp vegetable stock

Heat the oil in a wok over a medium to high heat.

Add the morning glory, the garlic, chilli, soya bean paste, stir-fry sauce and vegetable stock and stir for 1 minute.

Serve immediately.

A favourite side with that perfect blend of green goodness and a flavour burst from the garlic and chilli.

PAK CHOI & TENDERSTEM BROCCOLI VG

Serves 2

2 tbsp vegetable or rapeseed oil

2 tbsp crushed garlic

2 tsp crushed red chilli

2 pak choi, quartered

8 Tenderstem broccoli florets

30ml cold water

4 tbsp Stir-fry Sauce (see page 12)

2 tsp light soy sauce

2 pinches of cracked black pepper

Pour the oil into a wok over a medium to high heat. Add the crushed garlic and chilli and stir-fry for a minute. Add the pak choi, broccoli and cold water and stir-fry for 2 minutes. Now add the stir-fry sauce, soy sauce and black pepper and stir-fry for a final minute.

Remove from the heat and serve in two bowls.

Rice is an everyday staple in Thailand and often part of my daily diet here in the UK too. I love the subtle hint of flavour from the coconut in this dish. So simple, so satisfying.

COCONUT RICE VG

Serves 2

380g jasmine rice
6 tbsp granulated sugar
1 tsp salt
180ml coconut milk

Wash the rice in cold running water three times, draining the starchy water each time. For best results put the washed rice in a rice cooker with water in a 1:3 water-to-rice ratio. Cook on the white rice setting. When it's done, let the rice sit in the rice cooker for 10–20 minutes, then gently fluff with a spoon.

If you don't have a rice cooker put 200g of washed rice into a medium-size saucepan with 400g of cold water. Cook over a medium to high heat for 7–8 minutes and then use a fork or chopstick to stir the rice well, pour out any excess water so that the rice is just covered in the remaining water and continue cooking over a low heat with the lid on for another 4–5 minutes. Fully drain the rice.

Add the sugar, salt and coconut-milk to a saucepan and bring to the boil over a medium heat until the sugar and salt have completely dissolved. Remove from the heat.

Place the cooked jasmine rice in a bowl and add the thick coconut milk mixture and mix gently together. The coconut rice is now ready to serve.

In Thailand this is always eaten with your hands and the soft, sticky rice is squeezed between your fingers.

STICKY RICE vg

Serves 2

400g sticky rice
400ml water

Rice cooker method

Wash the rice in cold running water three times, draining the starchy water each time.

Put the washed rice and water in a rice cooker and cook on the white rice setting.

When it's done, let the rice sit in the rice cooker for 10–20 minutes, then gently fluff with a spoon.

Saucepan method

If you don't have a rice cooker put 400g washed rice into a medium-size saucepan with 800g cold water. Cook over a medium to high heat for 7–8 minutes and then use a fork or chopstick to stir the rice well. Pour out any excess water so that the rice is just covered in the remaining water and continue cooking over a low heat with the lid on for another 4–5 minutes. Fully drain the rice.

Bamboo steamer method

Wash the rice in cold running water three times, draining the starchy water away each time. Soak the rice overnight – for 400g use 1200ml water. When ready to cook, drain the rice and place it in the bamboo basket and cover with the lid. Fill the pot below with 2 litres of boiling water.

Steam the rice for 25–30 minutes.
Serve immediately.

I've always found this a kid-friendly dish, especially when little ones aren't in the mood to eat. It's a great way of sneaking a few extra ingredients into their meal!

EGG-FRIED RICE v

Serves 2

4 tbsp vegetable or rapeseed oil

2 tbsp frozen sweetcorn

2 tbsp frozen peas

1 small carrot, peeled and diced

2 eggs, beaten

380g cooked jasmine rice

2 pinches of salt

4 pinches of granulated sugar

2 pinches of cracked black pepper

Pour the oil into a wok over a medium to high heat. Add the sweetcorn, peas and carrot and stir-fry for 1 minute. Add the eggs and cook for 1 minute. Now add the cooked jasmine rice, salt, sugar and black pepper and toss it in the wok, ensuring the egg and vegetables are thoroughly mixed.

Remove from the heat and serve immediately.

Roti is a popular late-night snack in street-food markets across Thailand, often enjoyed as a sweet treat with sugar or condensed milk, but it's also perfect for mopping up delicious sauces. More polite than licking the bowl, too!

ROTI VG

Makes 8

250–300g wholewheat flour
1 tsp salt
2 tbsp vegetable or rapeseed oil,
   plus extra for greasing
235ml room temperature water

Whisk 250g of the flour with the salt in a large mixing bowl. Add the oil and stir it in until the flour looks sandy. Add the water and mix to make a shaggy dough.

Knead the dough for 10 minutes using your hands or a stand mixer fitted with the dough hook. Add more flour as necessary to make a soft but not sticky dough.

Drizzle some oil into a bowl and roll the dough ball in the bowl to coat it in oil. Cover and set aside to rest for at least 30 minutes but ideally more than 1 hour.

Turn out the dough onto a floured surface, divide into 8 pieces and roll each piece into a ball. Take one piece (leave the rest covered with a tea towel), flatten it with your palm to make a disc, then roll it out into a thin circle about 18–20cm in diameter. Repeat with the remaining dough balls.

Heat a dry frying pan over a medium to high heat. Brush any flour from the surface of a roti, then place it in the pan. Cook until the top of the dough just starts to look dry, then flip the roti. Brush the top with a thin layer of oil. Let the second side cook until it has light brown spots, then flip the roti again. Brush the second side with oil.

Continue cooking the roti until both sides have browned and formed black spots, flipping once or twice as needed. You can help the centre puff up by pressing the dough with a cloth or kitchen paper, or a spatula.

Wrap the cooked roti in a tea towel to steam and soften for 5 minutes (or just while you cook the remaining roti). Repeat until you've cooked all the roti – you should have 8 in total. Serve alongside curries (see pages 90–111) for dipping.

picture overleaf

SOMETHING SWEET

While our savoury dishes in Thailand are renowned
for their powerful flavours, our desserts are by
contrast delicate and subtle. A hint of sweetness
to round off a bold and exotic feast.

A traditional dessert enjoyed across Thailand – sometimes made with fresh mangoes gathered straight off the tree!

MANGO STICKY RICE PUDDING VG

Serves 2

380g sticky rice
380ml water
150g white sugar
1 tsp salt
300ml canned or fresh coconut milk
2 ripe mangoes, sliced

Wash the rice in cold running water three times, draining the starchy water each time.

Cook the rice with the water according to the packet instructions or use the methods listed on page 143. When it's done, let the rice sit for 10–20 minutes, then gently fluff with a spoon.

Add the sugar, salt and coconut milk to a saucepan and bring to the boil over a medium to high heat. Cook until the sugar and salt have completely dissolved, then remove from heat.

Place the cooked sticky rice in a bowl, add the thick coconut milk mixture and mix gently together. Leave to cool.

When ready to serve, divide the sticky coconut rice between two bowls and top with the sliced mango.

Not every dish needs to be complicated to be delicious and this straightforward dessert requires just a handful of ingredients and is very popular in Thailand.

KLAUI BUAT CHI – PLANTAIN & COCONUT DESSERT v

Serves 2

450ml canned or fresh coconut milk
150g granulated sugar
Pinch of salt
4 plantain (or bananas), quartered
1 tsp vanilla extract
Drizzle of honey (optional)

Pour the coconut milk into a saucepan over a medium heat, add the sugar and salt and bring to the boil.

Add the plantain or bananas along with vanilla extract and continue to cook until the plantain is soft. Remove from the heat and leave to cool to room temperature.

Serve warm or cold, with a drizzle of honey, if you like.

Simple and indulgent, this is a good go-to when you're craving something sweet. In some parts of Thailand we add longan fruit – it's similar to lychee, just more intensely sweet.

COCONUT STICKY RICE WITH PEACH VG

Serves 2

380g sticky rice
380ml water
450ml canned or fresh coconut milk
145g palm sugar (or soft brown sugar)
1 tsp salt
4 ripe peaches or papayas, sliced
Sprigs of fresh mint or Thai basil, to garnish (optional)

Wash the rice in cold running water three times, draining the starchy water each time.

Cook the rice with the water according to the packet instructions or use any methods listed on page 143. When it's done, let the rice sit for 10–20 minutes, then gently fluff with a spoon.

Meanwhile, place the coconut milk in a heavy saucepan over a medium heat and cook until hot, but do not boil. Add the sugar and salt and stir to dissolve completely.

When the sticky rice is tender, turn it out into a bowl and pour 225ml of the hot coconut milk over the top, reserving the rest. Stir to mix the liquid into the rice, then leave it to stand for 20 minutes–1 hour to allow the flavours to blend.

To serve individually, place an oval mound of sticky rice on each dessert plate alongside the sliced peaches (or papaya) and remaining coconut milk as desired. Decorate with a sprig of mint or basil if you wish.

BANANA LEAVES WITH STICKY RICE & BLACK BEANS VG

Serves 2

380g sticky rice

380ml water

255g palm sugar (or soft brown sugar)

1 tsp salt

450ml coconut milk

4 banana leaves

2 tablespoons canned black beans

String to tie parcels

Wash the rice in cold running water three times, draining the starchy water each time.

Cook the rice with the water according to the packet instructions or use any method listed on page 143. When it's done, let the rice sit for 10–20 minutes, then gently fluff with a spoon.

Add the sugar, salt and coconut milk to a saucepan and bring to the boil over a medium heat. Cook until the sugar and salt have completely dissolved, then remove from heat.

Place the cooked sticky rice in a bowl, add the thick coconut milk mixture and mix gently together. Leave to cool.

For each dessert, put a banana leaf on top of another banana leaf and then spread 3 tablespoons of the coconut sticky rice on top. Add 1 tablespoon of black beans to the middle and cover with another layer of 3 tablespoons of the coconut sticky rice.

Fold the banana leaves into parcels and tie with string to secure, then steam in a bamboo steamer basket or steamer pot for 15–20 minutes.

Serve hot or cold on round plates.

picture overleaf

Nothing beats fried banana fritters from a Thai street-food vendor, but this recipe comes close!

FRIED BANANA FRITTERS v

Serves 2

200g self-raising flour
2 tsp bicarbonate of soda
2 eggs
300ml milk, whole, semi-skimmed or coconut
225ml vegetable or rapeseed oil
2 ripe bananas, peeled and halved lengthways

To serve
4 tbsp clear honey
4 scoops of vanilla ice cream

Put the flour and bicarbonate of soda in a mixing bowl, stir together and make a well in the centre. Add the eggs and half the milk and mix well to form a smooth batter. Gradually beat in the remaining milk.

Pour the oil into a wok or deep saucepan over a medium to high heat.

Dip the banana pieces in the batter, then gently lower into the hot oil and fry until golden brown. Remove and drain on paper towels.

Serve with honey and/or ice cream.

The beauty of this dessert is in the contrasts! The pale pudding against the deep, ruby compote and the mild coconut flavour with the sweet sharpness of the berries.

COCONUT PUDDING WITH BERRY COMPOTE VG

Serves 2

Vegetable or rapeseed oil, for greasing
150g desiccated coconut
3 cardamom pods
500ml just-boiled water
500ml fresh or canned coconut milk
5 tbsp cornflour
65g granulated sugar
Pinch of salt
Sprigs of fresh mint, to garnish

For the berry compote
200g mixed berries
Juice of ½ lemon
60g maple syrup or granulated sugar

To make the compote, put the berries and lemon juice in a medium saucepan over a medium to high heat and cook for 3–4 minutes. Bring the mixture to the boil, then reduce the heat slightly and cook for a further 2–3 minutes, occasionally pressing the berries so they release more of their juices (though there's no need to mash them fully). Add the maple syrup (or sugar) towards the end of the cooking time and stir well. Adjust the amount of lemon juice and/ or sweetener at any time. Remove from the heat and either serve the fruit compote immediately or leave to cool and use later.

Grease two 7cm moulds or ramekins with oil.

Put the coconut and cardamom pods in a food processor or blender, add the just-boiled water and blend well.

If using fresh coconut milk, strain it through a sieve lined with a muslin cloth into a large bowl. If using canned coconut milk, pour it directly into the bowl. Add the cornflour, sugar and salt and whisk well, making sure there are no lumps.

Transfer the mixture to a large, deep pan over a low heat, stirring constantly until it thickens. When the mixture starts to thicken and turns glossy, that is the right consistency; overcooking it will make hard puddings and undercooking it will make it sticky and difficult to set. Pour the mixture into the prepared moulds. Leave to cool completely, then chill for 2 hours in the freezer to set fully.

Remove from the freezer a few minutes before serving to defrost slightly and serve with the berry compote, garnished with mint.

We were a little sceptical about putting a chocolate dessert on the menu in our restaurants, but chocolate has no national boundaries – and we've added a Thai flavour twist on this classic with the ginger and lime leaves.

THAI MELTING HEART CHOCOLATE FONDANTS v

Makes 6

100g unsalted butter, plus extra for greasing

10g cocoa powder, plus extra for dusting

100g dark chocolate

2 eggs

70g caster sugar

1 tsp freshly chopped ginger

4 makrut lime leaves, finely sliced

60g plain flour

½ tsp baking powder

Strawberries and whipped cream or vanilla
    ice cream, to serve (optional)

Lightly butter mini pudding basins (approx. 8cm wide x 6cm deep), dust with cocoa powder and place in the fridge.

Half-fill a large saucepan with water, then place a small saucepan containing the chocolate inside the larger pan with the water and heat gently. When the chocolate has melted, add the butter, then remove from the heat and mix together.

Whisk together the eggs and sugar. Once the mixture is pale, creamy and fluffy, fold in the melted chocolate, ginger and lime leaves. Add the flour, cocoa and baking powders and continue to fold until evenly combined.

Divide the mixture between the six pudding basins, leaving a 1cm gap at the top, and chill for about 1 hour. About 45 minutes into their chilling time, preheat the oven to 210°C.

Remove the pudding basins from the fridge and cook for 6–8 minutes until the tops resemble biscuits and are just beginning to crack.

Serve the fondants warm. Turn the fondants out of the basins onto plates or into bowls. They are delicious with strawberries and lightly whipped cream or vanilla ice cream.

Mango has such a gentle and obliging flavour, so you can get really creative with it. This ice cream is delicate and light – perfect to round off a meal with a hint of sweetness.

MANGO
ICE CREAM VG

Makes 1 litre

5 medium ripe mangoes (or 640g
    canned mango pulp)
360ml coconut cream
Juice of ½ lime
60g maple syrup
½ tsp salt
Coconut flakes or desiccated coconut,
    to serve (optional)

Wash and peel the mangoes. Then use a knife to cut the flesh away from the seed. Use a fork or spoon to scrape the seed and remove as much flesh as possible. You can do this straight into a food processor, or first into a bowl, whichever is easiest for you.

If you're using canned mango, then skip this step.

Add the mango flesh and all the remaining ingredients except the coconut to a food processor and blend into a smooth, creamy mango purée. This may take some time, so be patient. You want it to be ultra-smooth, so you don't have any 'bits' in your mango ice cream. Add a little more maple syrup or lime juice to suit your taste. Transfer to a freezerproof container and freeze for up to 1 month.

Serve scoops of ice cream sprinkled with coconut flakes or desiccated coconut, as you like.

We can't get enough of this delicious ice cream with its sweet nuttiness – there's always the temptation to have one last little mouthful!

PEANUT BUTTER ICE CREAM v

Makes 750ml (6 scoops)

240g smooth peanut butter
100g granulated sugar
2 pinches of fine sea salt (or kosher salt)
2 tsp vanilla extract
240ml whole milk
240ml single cream
240ml double cream

Using a hand-held mixer, cream the peanut butter, sugar, salt and vanilla in a large bowl until smooth. Add half the milk and single cream and beat on low speed until well mixed. Add the remaining milk and single cream and all the double cream and whisk by hand – if you try to use your mixer you will end up splattering it all over the kitchen.

Pour the mixture into an ice-cream machine and process for 25–30 minutes. The ice cream will be on the soft side but can be eaten right away or put into the freezer to harden for a couple of hours.

If you don't have an ice-cream maker, pour the mixture into a freezer-safe container and freeze for 45 minutes. As it starts to freeze near the edges, remove and stir vigorously to break up any frozen sections, then return to the freezer. Continue to check and stir as it freezes every 30 minutes. It will take 2–3 hours to be ready.

Stored in an airtight container, the ice cream will keep for at least a week in the freezer.

DRINKS

With so many delicious Thai fruits, herbs and spices to experiment with, we've had much fun (and a few giggles too, I admit!) creating our cocktail recipes – some with a Thai twist on a western classic and some based on infamous home-grown tipples like Thai Sabai, which you'll find in every bar in Bangkok!

The word sabai encompasses a whole Thai mindset and roughly translates as 'being comfortable, taking it easy, feeling relaxed'. Very appropriate for how you feel after this moreish cocktail.

THAI SABAI vg

Makes 1

50ml Mekhong (or rum of choice)

50ml lime juice

50ml Sugar Syrup (see below)

10 sweet basil leaves

25ml soda water

For the sugar syrup

100ml water

100g granulated sugar

½ small red chilli, sliced (optional)

To garnish

Basil sprig

Wedge or slice of lime

To make the sugar syrup, pour the water into a saucepan, add the sugar (and chilli if making a chilli sugar syrup) and bring to the boil. Boil for 30 seconds, then remove from the heat and leave to cool. Store in a jar in the fridge for up to a week. If you've made the Chilli Sugar Syrup, strain before using.

Pour the remaining ingredients into a cocktail shaker, except the soda water, add 3 ice cubes and shake hard. Pour straight into a rocks glass. Top with the soda water and garnish with a basil sprig and lime wedge.

Originally known as our 'Strawberry Mum-osa' when it first appeared in our restaurants as a Mother's Day Special. We had to include it, as it went down a treat.

STRAWBERRY MIMOSA VG

Makes 1

25ml vodka
25ml strawberry syrup
50ml prosecco of choice
Strawberry, to garnish

Add the vodka and syrup to a champagne flute, top up with the prosecco and stir.

Decorate the rim with a strawberry slice.

We love this due to its simplicity – there's no need for fussy measurements or bar tools. The combination of fizz and lychee is such a crowd-pleaser.

THAI BELLA BELLINI VG

Makes 1

25ml lychee liqueur, such as Kwai Feh, or strawberry liqueur
100ml prosecco

Pour the liqueur into a flute and top with the prosecco. Serve.

This one looks pretty, tastes delightful and is oh so very drinkable.

LYCHEE SILK VG

Makes 1

25ml vodka
25ml lychee liqueur, such as Kwai Feh
50ml jasmine tea
25ml Lychee Base Mix (see below)
Edible flower, to garnish

For the Lychee Base Mix
60ml lychee juice
60ml lemon juice
60ml Sugar Syrup (see page 172)
5ml lychee syrup

Mix the Lychee Base Mix ingredients together in a cocktail shaker.

Pour the remaining ingredients into the cocktail shaker, add 3 ice cubes and shake hard. Double strain into martini glass using a Hawthorne strainer and small sieve at the same time to stop any broken pieces of ice getting into the drink. Garnish with an edible flower and serve.

This is our version of a classic mojito, but ours has a little Thai sting of chilli which works so beautifully with the mango flavours. One of our bestsellers.

MANGO CHILLI MOSQUITO VG

Makes 1

35ml Mekhong (or white rum of choice)
75ml Mango Chilli Mix (see below)
12 mint leaves, plus a sprig, to garnish
50ml ginger ale

For the Mango Chilli Mix
50ml mango purée
10ml fresh lime juice
50ml Chilli Sugar Syrup (see page 172), strained

Mix the Mango Chilli Mix in a cocktail shaker.

Add the Mekhong, Mango Chilli Mix, mint leaves and ginger ale to the cocktail shaker, add 3 ice cubes and shake hard. Pour straight into a rocks glass. Top with the ginger ale and garnish with a mint sprig.

We love the subtle sweetness of this cocktail with the matcha liqueur, green tea and a hearty dash of tequila.

MATCHA-TINI v

Makes 1

25ml Tia Maria matcha cream liqueur
25ml silver (blanco) tequila, such as
  El Sueno Tequila Silver
50ml green tea
15ml Sugar Syrup (see page 172)
3 edible flowers, to garnish

Pour all the ingredients into a cocktail shaker, add 3 ice cubes and shake hard. Double strain into martini glass using a Hawthorne strainer and small sieve at the same time to stop any broken pieces of ice getting into the drink. Garnish with the edible flowers.

This is a great option for those who don't like overly sweet cocktails, it packs quite a fresh punch with the rum, prosecco, mint and lime.

RUM FIZZLER vg

Makes 1

25ml Mekhong (rum of choice)

20ml lime juice

20ml maple syrup

5 mint leaves

50ml prosecco

Lime twist, to garnish

Pour all the ingredients into a cocktail shaker, add 3 ice cubes and shake hard. Double strain into a martini glass using a Hawthorne strainer and small sieve at the same time to stop any broken pieces of ice getting into the drink. Top up with prosecco of your choice and garnish with a lime twist.

This refreshing, fruity gin cocktail is full of sunshine-y flavours such as passion fruit, orange and lime. Originally created as a vegan limited edition, it tastes too good not to include.

HIGH PASSION vg

Serves 1

35ml gin
10ml maple syrup
15ml lime juice
25ml orange juice
½ passion fruit to garnish

Add ice to a cocktail shaker, then add all the ingredients and shake hard!

Pour into a tall glass and garnish with ½ passion fruit.

This delicious mocktail is perfect for adults and children alike with its sweet Thai flavours of coconut, lime and pineapple.

SWEET JUNGLE COLADA VG

Makes 1

100ml Coconut Base Mix (see below)
50ml soda water
Mint sprig, to garnish

For the Coconut Base Mix
80ml coconut water
10ml pineapple Juice
25ml lime juice
30g granulated sugar
2g coconut syrup

To make the Coconut Base Mix, heat all the ingredients in a pan over a gentle heat until the sugar has dissolved. Set aside to cool.

Fill a tumbler with ice and pour over the Coconut Base. Top with the soda water and garnish with the mint sprig.

This is the tea version of a hug! Aromatic, comforting and flavoured with some fragrant spices – cloves, cardamom and star anise.

THAI TEA v

Serves 4

2 star anise

1 cinnamon stick

1 vanilla pod, split

1 litre water

6 Assam or Thai black teabags

2 tbsp agave syrup

6 tbsp sweetened condensed milk

4 tbsp whole milk

4 tbsp evaporated milk

Put the star anise, cinnamon stick and vanilla pod in a piece of muslin and tie at the top.

Bring the water to the boil in a large saucepan, now add the teabags and spices and gently boil for 5 minutes. Remove from the heat and set aside to steep for 3–4 minutes.

Stir in the agave syrup, sweetened condensed milk, whole milk and evaporated milk. Divide between four mugs and serve hot.

picture on page 197

The blend of coffee and the warming spices of nutmeg, cinnamon and cardamom works so well. Perfect for an afternoon pick-me-up or as a sweet indulgence after a filling meal.

SWEETLY SPICED ICED COFFEE v

Serves 2

6 tbsp strong freshly ground coffee

2 tsp ground cardamom

12 tbsp sweetened condensed milk

1 tsp ground cinnamon

Pinch of ground nutmeg

1 tsp vanilla essence

12 tbsp evaporated milk

Mix the coffee grounds with the ground cardamom and add to a cafetière. Add enough freshly boiled water for four cups of coffee and allow it to cool to lukewarm.

Add the sweetened condensed milk, cinnamon, nutmeg and vanilla to a jug. Mix with a spoon until completely combined and set aside.

Take four highball glasses and add 4 ice cubes to each glass.

Pour coffee into each glass, followed by equal amounts of the spice-infused, sweetened condensed milk and evaporated milk and stir with a spoon. Serve immediately.

This tea can also be served hot if you skip cooling the coffee and omit the ice.

picture overleaf

There's something about tea infused
with ancient Eastern spices that brings an
element of ritual with it. For me, it makes
that moment taken out of a busy day for
a cup of tea feel that bit more spoiling
and indulgent.

THAI ICED TEA v

Serves 4

2 star anise
2 green cardamom pods, smashed
2 cloves
1 litre water
4 teabags of Assam or Thai black tea
200g granulated sugar
150ml whole milk
120ml sweetened condensed milk

Put the star anise, cardamom pods and
cloves in a piece of muslin and tie at the top.

Bring the water to the boil in a large saucepan,
add the teabags, sugar and spices. Stir until
all the sugar dissolves. Gently boil the tea
for about 5 minutes, then remove from heat
and set aside to steep for at least 30 minutes.
If you need the tea to be more concentrated,
leave the teabags to steep for about 2 hours
for maximum flavour.

Remove the teabags and the spices and
leave the tea to cool to room temperature.
Store in the fridge for up to 2 days.

Fill four glasses with ice and pour in the Thai
tea, leaving some room to add the milk and
condensed milk.

INGREDIENTS

Thailand is abundant in natural resources and part of the joy of bringing Thai cooking to the UK is the opportunity to introduce some of these wonderful, flavour-enhancing herbs, spices and vegetables. Increasingly, even the most exotic Thai ingredients are becoming widely available but for your cooking ease, we've offered substitutions below too.

INGREDIENTS LIST:

Jicama

Jicama is a root vegetable that has a fresh, apple-like crunch and gentle flavour. Apple can be used as a good substitution here.

Concentrated Tamarind Juice

Concentrated tamarind juice is made from a sour, dark, sticky fruit that grows in a pod on a tamarind tree. It's available in some supermarkets and online.

Fish Sauce

A staple ingredient that brings a savoury, rich, umami flavour to many iconic Thai dishes. Widely available in supermarkets.

Fried Onions

Crispy fried onions are readily available in supermarkets, perfect for adding flavour and texture without the hassle of making your own.

Sriracha Sauce

Sriracha is a hot sauce that originated in Thailand and is made from a paste of chilli peppers, distilled vinegar, garlic, sugar and salt. It's widely available in supermarkets.

Rice Flakes (Kuay Jab recipe page 44)

For the Kuay Jab recipe we used 'rice flakes,' which are large rice-noodle squares and are available from Asian supermarkets or online. Please note: these should not be confused with other 'rice flake' products, which are small grains of rice noodles (that look a bit like porridge oats). You can also substitute the rice flakes with flat, 10mm-wide rice noodle sticks, which are widely available, without compromising the enjoyment of the dish.

Makrut lime leaves

An intense citrus flavour, lime leaves are widely available in supermarkets.

Lemongrass

Fresh lemongrass stalks have a distinctive, fragrant lemony scent and flavour and are available in most supermarkets.

Green Papaya

Green papaya is basically unripe papaya and is readily available in Asian supermarkets. As an alternative you could use swede – peeled and grated – as this is equally neutral in flavour and will hold the salad well without making the dish too wet.

Holy Basil

This herb has a slightly peppery, liquorice flavour in contrast to the sweeter Thai Basil. If you can't get hold of it, regular basil provides a good flavour substitute.

Ruby Noodles

We use beetroot noodles in our restaurants with their gorgeous, all-natural red colour. Widely available from major supermarkets, they are suitable for vegetarians and vegans.

Charcoal Noodles

A little less readily available than beetroot noodles but stocked in some major supermarkets. These noodles look so striking with their dark and moody colouring, achieved from vegetable charcoal. A great plant-based option.

Chillies

Everyone has their own spice tolerance, so tweak the recipes to suit yours. The chilli quantities in our recipes include the seeds but please remove these if you prefer less fire!

Chilli Paste

We like Mae Ploy Chilli Paste, which is available in many major supermarkets and online, but feel free to add your own favourite chilli paste to suit your tastes.

Thai Basil

Thai Basil has a sweet, anise quality. It is readily available from supermarkets. Other basils can be used as a substitute but will have a subtle effect on the flavour, so make sure you adapt and taste.

Galangal

Galangal is a spice closely related to ginger but with a slightly sharper and more peppery taste. Ginger makes a good substitution, though galangal is now widely available in supermarkets.

ACKNOWLEDGMENTS

Our first ever cookbook has been a long time in the dreaming and planning stages. It's been a true labour of love and collaboration and we'd like to acknowledge and thank the following for their time, effort and commitment:

All of our Giggling Squid chefs, led by Agnelo Pereira and Wiwat Kaewhanam for the creation and development of the recipes.

A huge thanks also to Hannah Johnson and Lezanne Clannachan for pulling the content together and finding the many words to bring our dishes to life.

Much gratitude also to the team at Ebury, with special thanks to Elizabeth Bond for helping us create a cookbook we are so very proud of.

And of course, my love and thanks to Andy and our three children for being my favourite food tasters – always willing, always honest.

INDEX

Note: page numbers
in **bold** refer to illustrations.

9

Ebury Press an imprint of Ebury Publishing,

One Embassy Gardens, 8 Viaduct Gdns, Nine Elms London SW11 7BW

Ebury Press is part of the Penguin Random House group of companies whose addresses can be found at global.penguinrandomhouse.com

Penguin Random House UK

Text © Ebury Press 2022
Photography © Ebury Press 2022
Design © Ebury Press 2022

Photography: Haarala Hamilton
Food Stylist: Jake Fenton
Assistant Food Stylist: Hattie Baker
Prop Stylist: Daisy Shayler-Webb
Design: Studio Polka
Production: Rebecca Jones
Publishing Director: Elizabeth Bond

Giggling Restaurants Ltd have asserted their right to be identified as the author

First published by Ebury Press in 2022
This edition published in 2022

www.penguin.co.uk

A CIP catalogue record for this book is available from the British Library

ISBN 9781529195606

Printed and bound Bell & Bain Ltd, UK

The authorised representative in the EEA is Penguin Random House Ireland, Morrison Chambers, 32 Nassau Street, Dublin D02 YH68

Penguin Random House is committed to a sustainable future for our business, our readers and our planet. This book is made from Forest Stewardship Council® certified paper.